Cambridge Elements ≡

Elements in European Politics
edited by
Catherine De Vries
Bocconi University
Gary Marks
University of North Carolina at Chapel Hill and European University Institute

CRISIS POLICYMAKING IN THE EU

The COVID-19 Crisis and the Refugee Crisis 2015–16 Compared

Hanspeter Kriesi
European University Institute

Shaftesbury Road, Cambridge CB2 8EA, United Kingdom

One Liberty Plaza, 20th Floor, New York, NY 10006, USA

477 Williamstown Road, Port Melbourne, VIC 3207, Australia

314–321, 3rd Floor, Plot 3, Splendor Forum, Jasola District Centre,
New Delhi – 110025, India

103 Penang Road, #05–06/07, Visioncrest Commercial, Singapore 238467

Cambridge University Press is part of Cambridge University Press & Assessment,
a department of the University of Cambridge.

We share the University's mission to contribute to society through the pursuit of
education, learning and research at the highest international levels of excellence.

www.cambridge.org
Information on this title: www.cambridge.org/9781009549455

DOI: 10.1017/9781009549462

First published 2024

A catalogue record for this publication is available from the British Library

ISBN 978-1-009-54945-5 Hardback
ISBN 978-1-009-54949-3 Paperback
ISSN 2754-5032 (online)
ISSN 2754-5024 (print)

Additional resources for this publication at www.cambridge.org/kriesi-resources

Crisis Policymaking in the EU

The COVID-19 Crisis and the Refugee Crisis 2015–16 Compared

Elements in European Politics

DOI: 10.1017/9781009549462
First published online: December 2024

Hanspeter Kriesi
European University Institute

Author for correspondence: Hanspeter Kriesi, hanspeter.kriesi@eui.eu

Abstract: This Element compares crisis-specific policymaking, its causes and consequences, at the two levels of the EU polity during the COVID-19 and the refugee crisis 2015–16. In both crises, EU policymaking responded to exogenous pressure and was dominated by executive decision-making. Still, it also differed in three critical aspects: it was much more salient, consensual, and effective during the COVID-19 than the refugee crisis. The present study accounts for both similarities and differences, which it attempts to explain by features of the nature of the crises. The key argument of the study is that the policymaking process during crises is, to a large extent, determined by the crisis situation – the crisis-specific functional problem pressure, the institutional context (of the EU polity), and the corresponding political pressure at the origin of a given crisis. This title is also available as Open Access on Cambridge Core.

Keywords: crisis policymaking, EU polity, COVID-19, refugee crisis 2015–16, comparison

ISBNs: 9781009549455 (HB), 9781009549493 (PB), 9781009549462 (OC)
ISSNs: 2754-5032 (online), 2754-5024 (print)

Contents

An online appendix for this publication can be accessed at www.cambridge.org/kriesi-resources

1 Introduction

This Element compares crisis-specific policymaking and its causes and consequences at the two levels of the EU polity during the COVID-19 crisis and the refugee crisis 2015–16. Crisis policymaking in the EU was in some respects similar during the two crises – it responded to exogenous pressure and was dominated by executive decision-making in both crises. Still, it also differed in three critical aspects: It was much more salient, consensual, and effective during the COVID-19 crisis than during the refugee crisis. The present study accounts for both similarities and differences, which it attempts to explain by features of the crisis situations or, in other words, by the nature of the two crises. The key argument of the study is that the policymaking process during crises is, to a large extent, determined by the crisis situation – the crisis-specific functional problem pressure (substantive, temporal, and spatial), the institutional context (of the EU polity), and the corresponding political pressure at the origin of a given crisis and throughout its subsequent development. The argument also takes into account that crises are multifaceted phenomena that concern multiple policy domains, which means that the crisis situation may vary in policy-specific ways within a given crisis. The argument is structuralist, but it leaves room for actor strategies to make a difference within the constraints imposed by the crisis situation.

The structuralist argument is particularly adapted to crises such as the two compared here, which constitute exogenous shocks that unexpectedly hit a polity, creating great urgency and uncertainty. In the case of the refugee crisis, this was not the first crisis of its kind, nor was the turn of events in the late summer of 2015 entirely unexpected. But it still hit the EU and its member states with full force (Kriesi et al. 2024: 3). The crucial event that illustrates the impact of exogenous pressure occurred on September 4 2015, when thousands of asylum seekers decided to leave the central train station in Budapest, where they had been stuck for some time, and to march on along the Hungarian highways in their stated goal to reach German soil. The Hungarian government, all too pleased by the asylum seekers' decision to move on, facilitated their arduous trek toward the Austrian border by sending buses to accommodate them and bring them to the border. Faced with the prospect of the approaching caravan, the Austrian government urgently sought the help of the German government. It was during the night of this Saturday in September 2015, under the immediate pressure of the refugees proceeding toward the Austrian–Hungarian border, that the German Chancellor took the critical decision to admit asylum seekers into Germany, although they had already passed through several other member states of the Union.

In the case of the COVID-19 crisis, the first significant outbreak of infections was observed in the North of Italy on February 20. Rapidly, the virus spread across Italy and Europe. By the end of March, Italy counted more than 100,000 cases and no less than 10,000 coronavirus deaths. The nightly convoy of military trucks removing coffins with the dead from Bergamo rendered the impact of the exogenous shock visible across Europe. At the same time, most other European countries were greatly affected as well. An even greater wave followed the first shock wave in the fall of 2020, and yet a third wave occurred one year later. Moreover, the COVID-19 crisis also proved to be an economic shock that led to the most severe global economic contraction since the 1930s. After the first lockdowns, economic activity broke down across Europe. Following up on earlier severe drops on March 9 (Black Monday I) and 12 (Black Thursday), the stock market crashed on March 16 (Black Monday II), signaling the beginning of the COVID-19 recession.

Crises are generally highly salient public events, but the COVID-19 crisis is in a class of its own. It was one of the biggest news stories ever (The Economist, 19/12/2020). Only the world wars rival COVID-19's share of news coverage. The exceptional character of the COVID-19 crisis needs to be underlined since its extraordinary salience influences every aspect of the crisis-related policymaking process. The European refugee crisis 2015–16 ("the refugee crisis") was also highly salient. Still, crisis policymaking related to this crisis did not dominate the policymaking process in the EU to the same extent as during the COVID-19 crisis. The greater salience of the COVID-19 crisis is a result of its existential, unexpected, novel, and encompassing character. It posed an unprecedented threat to the health of the European populations and their economies. The refugee crisis was less existential for the populations at large; it was more familiar since it was not the first crisis of its sort in the European context, and it was less encompassing (affecting only some member states, but not others). At the same time, the COVID-19 crisis was less contentious than the refugee crisis, which, arguably, is also related to the encompassing existential threat it posed and to the extraordinary moment of urgency and uncertainty that occurred when the crisis hit the EU member states more or less simultaneously in early March 2020. These differences in the crisis situations of the two crises go a long way in explaining why EU problem-solving during the COVID-19 crisis was much more consensual and successful than during the refugee crisis of 2015–16. Concerning the COVID crisis, positive assessments of the EU's crisis management prevail in the literature (Anghel and Jones 2023; Fabbrini 2022; Quaglia and Verdun 2023; Rhodes 2021; Wolff and Ladi 2020), while the literature is much more critical about the limited, minimum common denominator solutions which characterized the crisis management during the refugee crisis (e.g., Biermann et al. 2017; Jones, Kelemen, and Meunier 2021; Lavenex 2018).

This study speaks to the European integration literature and, in particular, its treatment of the series of crises (see, for example, Schimmelfennig 2021; Genschel and Jachtenfuchs 2018; Genschel and Jachtenfuchs 2021; Hooghe and Marks 2019; Jones, Kelemen, and Meunier 2021; Schimmelfennig 2018). It focuses on the policymaking process, its determinants, and consequences, building on Ferrera, Kriesi, and Schelkle (2024) and Ferrara and Kriesi (2022). In contrast to the latter paper, however, the goal is not to show how the various integration theories contribute to explaining different crises but to propose and test a framework that systematically compares crisis policymaking in the EU. The study claims that understanding how policymaking works at the two levels of the EU polity is crucial for understanding the functioning of the EU, especially in times of crisis. If "Europe will be forged in crisis, and will be the sum of the solutions adopted for those crises," as Jean Monnet (1978: 417) claimed, it depends very much on the European policymakers' response to the crises, whether they contribute to Europe's resilience or undermine it. And the policymakers' response, in turn, is very much shaped by the largely exogenously determined nature of the crises.

In stressing the impact of the various parameters of the crisis situation, the study also speaks to the emergency politics literature, which suggests that crises may be fabricated and manipulated by interested parties (e.g., White 2020). This literature sees crisis situations not so much as the operating environment imposed on policymakers facing an exogenous shock but as the outcome of a calculated politics of exception fostered by institutional incentives and deliberate strategies. I concede that policymakers use strategies of "crisisification" (Rhinard 2019), i.e., exploit crises to increase support for the government and its policy agendas (Boin, 't Hart, and McConnell 2009; Rauh, Bes, and Schoonvelde 2020), and that political actors actively cue their followers in crises just as they do in regular times (e.g., Kriesi and Vrânceanu 2023; Zaller 1992). As stated by constructivists more generally, events can, indeed, be constituted by interpretative agents (Alexander-Shaw, Ganderson, and Kyriazi 2023: 9). However, the framework of this study puts political entrepreneurship into the context of functional problem pressure and institutional constraints and the way they shape political pressure exerted by the public agenda. Against the skeptic who would say that what counts as a crisis depends on your political views,[1] this study argues that the constraints imposed by the crisis situation are such that political views become largely secondary in defining a crisis. It argues

---

[1] An argument made by one of the anonymous reviewers of this study.

that to understand policymaking during crises such as the two compared here, it is crucial to start from these constraints and study how they shape the reactions of policymakers.

The study also relates to the policy process literature, especially the punctuated equilibrium theory (Baumgartner, Jones, and Mortensen 2014). This approach is closely related to crisis policymaking since it considers that "although generally marked by stability and incrementalism, political processes occasionally produce large-scale departures from the past" (p. 59). Crises occur, providing "windows of opportunity" for policy innovations. In crises, policymaking, according to this approach, shifts from parallel processing in issue-specific policy subsystems to serial processing by macro-political institutions and key executives, an idea that I take up in this study. Empirically, the punctuated equilibrium approach focuses on the agenda-setting phase of the policymaking process, as illustrated by the prodigious work of the comparative agenda-setting project (Baumgartner, Breunig, and Grossman 2019). This study extends the empirical focus to the entire policymaking process. It attempts to assess to what extent the two crises provided "windows of opportunity" for policymaking in the EU polity.

2 Theoretical Framework

Introduction

Three features of a crisis are commonly identified: threat, urgency, and uncertainty (see Alexander-Shaw, Ganderson, and Kyriazi 2023; Boin et al. 2005: 3–4; Ferrara and Kriesi 2022; Lipscy 2020). The *crisis situation* corresponds to an extraordinary moment of urgency and uncertainty that poses an immediate threat to the proper functioning of the policy domain concerned by the crisis and, if the threat is existential enough, to the population at large and the polity as a whole. Crisis situations are embedded in a context. They vary with the nature of the threat exerted by the crisis, the polity in which they occur, and the conflict structure that prevails in the polity. In the case of our two crises, the nature of the threat is given by the Syrian civil war and the large number of refugees it created and by the pandemic. A master tension between the supranational center and the member states characterizes the EU polity exposed to these threats (Ferrera, Kriesi, and Schelkle 2024). This tension gives rise to center–periphery conflicts between the supranational center and the member states, territorial conflicts between member states (transnational conflicts), and functional conflicts between pro-integrationist (cosmopolitan) and anti-integrationist (nationalist) social groups within member states.

Crisis situations, in turn, shape the crisis-specific policymaking processes, the policy output, the policy outcome, and broader implications for the polity at

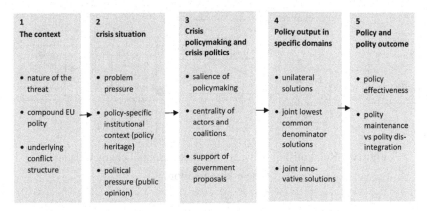

Figure 1 The analytical building blocks of the theoretical framework.
Source: Author's elaboration.

large.[2] Figure 1 presents the analytical building blocks of the argument. This study focuses on the link between crisis situation and crisis-specific policymaking and policy output. The essential claim of this study is that the crisis situation decisively shapes crisis-specific politics and policymaking, which then determines the policy output and effectiveness. The broader implications of crisis policymaking for the resilience of the polity will get little attention.

The discussion of the theoretical framework is divided into two sections: The first section introduces the concepts for the characterization of the crisis situation and describes the two crises studied here in terms of the relevant characteristics; the second section formulates expectations about the impact of the crisis situation on crisis-specific policymaking processes and their output.

The Crisis Situations

Figure 2 presents the relationship between the three elements of the crisis situation as proposed by this framework. Problem pressure comes first. It derives directly from the critical context, particularly the threat exerted by the crisis. Political pressure on the policymakers is partly due to problem pressure. However, it can also be created by political actors intent on exploiting the crisis for their purposes, as argued by the emergency politics literature and others. Alternatively, political pressure can be alleviated by political actors coming to the rescue of those directly exposed to problem pressure. In any case, the effect of problem pressure on political pressure is partly mediated by the institutional context. In the specific context of the EU polity, the effect of problem pressure

---

[2] The conceptual distinction between crisis situations and crisis outcomes is inspired by Charles Tilly's (1978: 189ff.) distinction between a revolutionary situation and revolutionary outcomes.

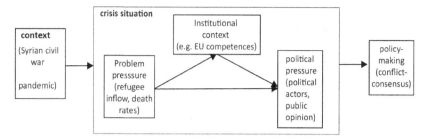

Figure 2 Relationship between the three essential characteristics of the crisis situation.

on political pressure at one level may be mediated by the institutional context at the other level – e.g., by EU authorities coming to the rescue of hard-hit member states and, thus, alleviating the political pressure exerted by the respective publics on their national governments. This means that problem pressure may be neither sufficient nor necessary for political pressure. In the final analysis, political pressure is a matter of perception and is not entirely structurally determined by problem pressure. Figure 2 presents the overall relationship between these basic characteristics of the crisis situation, which I discuss individually.

Problem Pressure

Problem pressure has substantive, temporal, and spatial aspects. In *substantive* terms, we can distinguish between the size or intensity of the threat exerted by the crisis and the policy domains concerned by the threat. The threat can be more or less existential, i.e., more or less threatening to the survival of existing institutional arrangements in a given policy domain or even the polity's survival (Jones, Daniel Kelemen, and Meunier 2021: 1526). The COVID-19 crisis differs from the refugee crisis in that it posed an existential threat, while the refugee crisis did not. Although the refugee crisis was considered the most severe threat to the survival of the EU by the European public before the COVID-19 crisis (Kriesi et al. 2024: 4 f.), the threat posed by this crisis to the populations of the EU member states was less existential than the threat of the COVID-19 pandemic. As already mentioned, the pandemic was an extremely salient shock that put the COVID-19 crisis in a class of its own. Moreover, several waves of this crisis were triggered by a renewed shock created by a new variant of the virus. The refugee crisis of 2015–16 was also triggered by a tremendous shock wave at the end of the summer of 2015 when the trek of hundreds of thousands of refugees traveled north on the Balkan route.

However, this shock was less directly threatening to the population's survival and the national economy. Moreover, it decreased considerably after the EU had concluded an agreement with Turkey in March 2016.

As for the policy domain, crises are multifaceted phenomena that may involve several policy domains and different types of policymakers. The two crises also differ in this respect. While the refugee crisis focused on border control, asylum policy, and integration policy – all elements of migration policy – the COVID-19 crisis was a double crisis: a public health and an economic crisis, which touched upon multiple policy domains. In terms of public health, lockdowns and border closures were distinguished from public health measures in the narrower sense of the term – the procurement of medical equipment (e.g., face masks, ventilators), testing, contact tracing, or quarantine measures, and the development and distribution of vaccines. In terms of the economy, macro-economic measures (monetary and fiscal policy) were to be distinguished from competition policy (the suspension of single market rules), industrial policy (liquidity guarantees or subsidies to companies), or social policy (unemployment insurance, furlough schemes, social assistance). As a result, the problem pressure was broader in *scope* and concerned many more policymakers in the COVID-19 crisis than in the refugee crisis.

In terms of *temporal* development, crisis situations can be distinguished according to the novelty of the crisis, the timing of the threat's origin (sudden and unexpected vs cumulative and expected threats), and the timing of its effects (immediate vs delayed) (see Pierson 2004: Chapter 3). There are new, unfamiliar crises, and recurrent crises. There are fast-moving crises resulting from an unexpected exogenous shock with direct consequences and slow-moving crises, which develop cumulatively and have delayed effects (Seabrooke and Tsingou 2019). If, as constructivists point out (Alexander-Shaw, Ganderson, and Kyriazi 2023), the interpretation of the defining moments of a crisis lies in the eye of the beholder, this applies to familiar and/or slow-moving crises in particular. In the novel and/or fast-moving cases, it is arguably more likely that policymakers are forced by the events they encounter to recognize the problem pressure and, as the events unfold, to devise an immediate policy response, which is likely to be heavily shaped by the crisis situation.

Regarding the timing of *effects*, the two crises resemble each other. Both were characterized by a moment of shock, which required a rapid, immediate response from the policymakers. However, they differ regarding the timing of the crisis's *origin*. While the COVID-19 crisis was a novel crisis that could not be foreseen, the refugee crisis was recurrent and could have been expected by policymakers. In the case of COVID-19, the crisis hit unexpectedly and very rapidly before the EU and its member states could prepare a proper joint response. To be sure, the EU convened the Health Security Committee (HSC) in January 2020, which then met ten times up to March 2, 2020. However, the first transnational political engagement on the crisis only occurred at the February 13 meeting of EU health ministers, shortly before the first cases occurred in Lombardy, Italy, on February 20. The economic impact of COVID-19 was first discussed only at a meeting of the Competitiveness Council on February 27, 2020, shortly before the rapid spread of the virus across the Union (Laffan 2023). The refugee crisis, by contrast, was not the first crisis of its kind, and the problem pressure had already increased before the crisis hit in earnest in late summer 2015. Asylum policy was already highly politicized before the crisis. Moreover, EU policymakers saw the crisis coming: The agenda-setting European Agenda for Migration of Spring 2015 was a response to the surge of Mediterranean arrivals but was also built on twenty-five years of policymaking experience (Geddes 2018). However, the intense politicization of asylum policy prevented policymakers from reacting decisively in anticipation of what was going to happen (Kriesi et al. 2024: 90 f.). Once they had decided to act, they could nevertheless fall back on a policy heritage that they had already applied to earlier crises (Geddes 2021).

In *spatial* terms, in the EU polity, it is essential that the *distribution of the threat among the member states* may vary from one crisis to the other. In this respect, we can distinguish between situations where member states are symmetrically or asymmetrically affected (Ferrara and Kriesi 2022). Arguably, the COVID-19 crisis was symmetric – a general public health crisis that hit all member states similarly. Even if the member states were not all equally prepared to come to terms with the crisis (Quaglia and Verdun 2023: 640), the fact that they were all hit by the pandemic created favorable conditions for joint management. The refugee crisis 2015–16, by contrast, hit the member states quite selectively: The Mediterranean frontline states (such as Greece and Italy) bore the brunt of the crisis, together with the open destination states (such as Germany and Sweden), where the secondary movements of the refugees ended up. Transit states (such as Hungary and Austria) were only temporarily affected. In contrast, closed destination states in Western Europe (such as France and the UK) and bystander states in Eastern Europe (such as Poland or the Baltic states) were hardly affected at all (Kriesi et al. 2021; Kriesi et al. 2024).

Policy-Specific Institutional Context

In the compound EU polity, member states usually struggle independently from each other. Still, in crises, especially the most hard-hit, member states turn to the EU and their fellow member states for help. As Milward (2000) famously claimed, from its beginnings, the EU was designed to come to the rescue of the nation-states. Furthermore, the nation-states, having become member states that understand their power and identity as dependent on belonging to a broader group or community (Bickerton 2012), expect the EU and the other member states to come to their rescue in crisis situations. We observe such a move in all acute crises. The chances of getting support depend on the policy-specific institutional context, which has a vertical and a horizontal dimension.

The *vertical* dimension refers to the *policy-specific competence distribution* between the EU and its member states. We can distinguish between policy domains that fall under the direct or (quasi-) exclusive competence of the EU and policy domains that remain (at least partially) within the remit of member states. Ferrara and Kriesi (2022) use the term "policy heritage" to refer to this dimension to emphasize the path dependency of the policy-specific power distribution. Jones, Kelemen, and Meunier (2021) refer to the "lock-in effect" of past policies. The accumulation of past policies generates specific repertoires of governance for the decision-makers but also imposes particular constraints on the EU authorities and member state governments (see Geddes 2021). In the COVID-19 crisis, the EU had a lot of competence in economic policy, which was concerned with preserving the single market (e.g., competition policy, state aid policy) and monetary policy (in the mandate of the European Central Bank). The EU shared competence with the member states in fiscal policy and had weak competence in public health and vaccination policy. In the refugee crisis, the EU shared competences in asylum policy with the member states, but the latter were entitled to call the final shots. In both crises, the member states ultimately decided on border control measures, given that the Schengen regime allows for temporary suspensions of the open border regime. However, the EU intervened much more in border control issues of the member states during the refugee crisis than in the COVID-19 crisis because of the different externalities for other member states created by the respective measures in the two crises (see next section).

The *horizontal* dimension of the policy-specific institutional context refers to the *transnational power relations* between the member states. In the EU polity, not all member states are alike; there are institutionalized power hierarchies. Member states have different vote endowments – depending on size – in the Council of the EU and various capacities to contribute to the common good. Large member states not only have a stronger position in the policymaking process than smaller ones but are also expected to make a more significant contribution to the common good (Thielemann 2018). Informally, larger states may also provide leadership to resolve the crisis. Thus, Germany and France, the EU's two largest countries, have often exercised joint leadership (Krotz and

Schramm 2022). On various occasions, they have played a pivotal role in European integration and decisively shaped EU policies and the EU polity.

However, crisis-induced power relations may modify the more or less institutionalized power hierarchy among member states due to an asymmetric distribution of the crisis incidence and its implications on the member state governments. According to the predictions of liberal intergovernmentalism (Moravcsik 1998), in an asymmetric crisis, the bargaining position of member states that suffer from asymmetrical crisis incidence will be undermined, while the bargaining position of the fortunate members will be reinforced. Thus, Germany's institutional position was strengthened during the Euro Area crisis since it was the main creditor to other member states. By contrast, Germany's position was undermined in the refugee crisis because it was hit hard by the crisis and was forced to solicit joint solutions. As a result of the crisis incidence, Germany's government was additionally weakened by intraparty conflicts in the senior governing party (CDU-CSU). A constrained government that desperately needs a joint solution at the EU level is unlikely to be able to put other member states under pressure. The fortunate members who do not seek an agreement will not be inclined to come to the aid of a member state whose government is divided over the joint proposals to be agreed upon. In contrast, given its capacity to deal with the pandemic, Germany was not more dependent on collaborative solutions than other member states in the COVID-19 crisis, which means that crisis-induced factors did not undermine its strong position.

As a result of the series of crises that have hit the EU in the past decade, a set of transnational *coalitions* have emerged, which structure the transnational power relations in policy domain-specific ways (see Fabbrini 2023). In addition to the German--French joint leadership coalition, these coalitions include the so-called solidarity coalition, consisting of the southern member states and France. These "letter-9 countries" demanded more solidarity, especially economically, early in the COVID-19 crisis. Then, there is the "sovereigntist" Visegrad 4 coalition (V4), composed of Hungary, Poland, the Czech Republic, and Slovakia. This coalition played a vital role in the peak period of the refugee crisis when it adamantly opposed the relocation scheme that the Commission, together with Germany, sought to impose. In the COVID-19 crisis, V4 consolidated due to the rule-of-law conditioning introduced in the ratification phase of the Resilience and Recovery Facility (RRF). The "Frugal 4," composed of the Netherlands, Austria, Denmark, Sweden, and, at times, Finland, constitute the fourth coalition (Verdun 2022). This coalition mobilized opposition to a generous RRF solution and favored more strict rule-of-law conditionality in the COVID-19 crisis. Finally, during the two crises, the UK was still an EU member, albeit one that had always been skeptical of EU solidarity and had previously opted out of joint solutions. In the refugee crisis, as a non-Schengen member state, it was hardly affected at all, and in the COVID-19 crisis, it opted out of joint vaccination procurement.

The policy-specific institutional context is also shaped by two national conditions – the *composition of the national government* and the *intensity of the new cultural cleavage in national politics*. The composition of the governments varies with the vicissitudes of the national electoral cycles in the member states, which are not aligned with the crisis shocks, and with the strength of the new cultural cleavage, which opposes cosmopolitans to nationalists.[3] Traditionally, governing parties have been more pro-European than opposition parties with no government experience (Hobolt and de Vries 2015). Incumbent parties are more likely to be mainstream parties, which typically hold more positive views about the EU (Hooghe, Marks, and Wilson 2002; De Vries and Hobolt 2020), and they are directly involved in EU decision-making and the implementation of EU-related policies, which enhances their understanding and support of EU policies. However, with the increasing importance of the new cleavage between cosmopolitans and nationalists, decidedly anti-European parties have been gaining in strength and have become governing parties in some member states. In Hungary and Poland, but also Italy for some time, they have even become the main governing parties – in Hungary since 2010, in Poland since the 2015 elections at the peak of the refugee crisis in fall of that year until fall 2023, and in Italy from summer 2018 to summer 2019.

Political Pressure

In EU politics, political pressure is exerted on supranational authorities and member state governments. The political pressure on the former mainly comes from individual member states or the transnational coalitions of member states. Given the high threshold of consensus requirements in EU intergovernmental decision-making, transnational coalitions can obtain disproportional power. This is especially true in asymmetric crises, such as the refugee crisis, where the fortunate member states have the incentive to constrain joint decision-making.

The governments of member states are generally exposed to political pressures from two sides – the EU polity on the one hand and domestic politics on

---

[3] This new cleavage has been labeled differently by different scholars: "GAL-TAN" (Hooghe, Marks, and Wilson 2002), "independence-integration" (Bartolini 2005), "integration-demarcation" (Kriesi et al. 2008, 2012), "universalism-communitarianism" (Bornschier 2010), "cosmopolitanism-communitarianism" (Zürn and Wilde 2016), "cosmopolitanism-parochialism" (Vries 2017), "transnational cleavage" (Hooghe and Marks 2018), and the cleavage between sovereignism and Europeanism (Fabbrini 2019: 62f).

the other. The political pressure from the EU polity comes from interventions by EU authorities and other member states in national policymaking. Such interventions may trigger the mobilization of national identities in an attempt to offer resistance. In asymmetric crises such as the refugee crisis, such interventions are more likely since member states are more likely to resort to unilateral policies, which violate EU policy or substitute for the lack of EU policy, with asymmetric externalities (e.g., in the form of secondary movements) for other member states. By contrast, in symmetric crises such as the COVID-19 crisis, solidarity between EU member states is likely to be enhanced by identity-based empathy and interdependence-based sympathy (Genschel and Jachtenfuchs 2021: 9). The common threat experienced by all member states is a powerful driver of expanded expectations of community (as argued by federalism as a theory of regional integration, e.g., McKay 2004). In the COVID-19 crisis, member states took unilateral action, too, but since they all had to confront the same challenge, they took similar measures. This means that the externalities were rather symmetrically distributed, and the member states could not mutually blame each other for their unilateral actions.

Domestic political pressure is, first of all, exerted by *public opinion*. Problem pressure creates crisis-specific public attention, which serves as the immediate driver of crisis-specific policymaking by the government. The government can hardly ignore high crisis-specific public attention. By contrast, the same public attention also constitutes a mobilization potential for all kinds of political actors, but especially for challenger and mainstream opposition parties and civil society organizations. Partisan mobilization can also create public attention by providing cues and frames for interpreting the crisis situation. Still, in the case of exogenous shocks like the two crises we are studying here, partisan mobilization is more likely to react to heightened public attention.

In addition, partisan mobilization is more or less constrained by the specific nature of the crisis. Thus, the COVID-19 crisis did not easily lend itself to partisan politicization since it did not match classic economic or cultural conflict lines that structure the national party systems. In particular, this crisis did not lend itself to mobilizing nationalist identities by the radical populist right, which is likely to undermine joint EU-level solutions. To the extent that parties politicized the COVID-19 crisis in later waves, they broadly framed it in traditional economic terms: The right promoted the opening up of the economy and the self-reliance of the citizens, while the left defended tighter lockdown measures (Rovny et al. 2022). Both the symmetric incidence of the crisis in all member states and the characteristics of a public health crisis that seemingly hit everybody in society in similar ways limited the possibilities for its exploitation by populist parties. There were other political actors – institutional actors (health and educational institutions, the national parliaments), civil society actors (business, trade unions, experts, think tanks, civil society organizations), as well as regional governments, which were mobilizing the interests of specific societal groups against the governments' unilaterally imposed emergency policies. However, these other actors did not politicize national identities since the EU policy conflicts hardly spilled over to the domestic level.

By contrast, the refugee crisis provided a golden opportunity for the radical populist right to mobilize nationalist identities and intensify its mobilization against immigration, its preferred terrain. Moreover, this crisis intervened at a moment when Europe's rising radical right had already highly politicized immigration issues. However, the pressure on the government was not only coming from the radical right but also from the mainstream opposition, which tried to pin the government into the corner by accusing it either of doing too little in coming to terms with asylum seeker flows (nationalist opposition) or of excesses and inhumane treatment of asylum seekers (humanitarian opposition from the left, joined by civil society). As regards the nationalist pressure, the electoral success of the radical right parties prompted mainstream parties to engage in strategic responses to fend off this electoral threat, often by shifting their programmatic position toward a more restrictive stance on immigration (Abou-Chadi and Krause 2020; Abou-Chadi, Cohen, and Wagner 2021). In extreme cases, such strategic positioning could play out within the government itself in the case of coalitions, especially grand coalitions (Engler, Bauer-Blaschkowski, and Zohlnhöfer 2019; Höhmann and Sieberer 2020). In sum, in the refugee crisis, the decision-makers at the national level, particularly, were highly exposed to the political pressure exerted by partisan opposition.

The Impact of the Crisis Situation on Policymaking and Policy Output

The dependent variables of this study are characteristics of policymaking and policy output that can be compared across crises. They include the salience of crisis-specific policymaking, the role (centrality) of the various actors in the policymaking process, policy support, and policy output. I discuss them one by one and formulate a series of hypotheses for each one of them. These hypotheses focus on the following aspects (between parentheses are mentioned the initials of the corresponding hypotheses):

- Crisis policymaking in general (H1-4)
- General crisis-specific effects (H1a-4a)
- Phase-specific effects (H1b-4b)
- Pressure-specific effects (H1c-4c)

- Policy-specific effects (H1d-4d)
- Actor-specific effects at EU (H1e-4e) and member state level (H1f-4f)
- Country-specific effects (H1g-4g).

The Salience of Crisis-Specific Policymaking

The exogenous shock of the crisis forces the policymakers to respond immediately, i.e., the salience of crisis-specific policymaking increases sharply in reaction to the exogenous shock. The exogenous shock gives rise to "fast-burning" emergency politics, when governing authorities react quickly to avoid disaster. At both levels of the EU polity, policymakers must respond and cannot escape the problem and political pressure of such shocks (H1). However, the impact is expected to be more pronounced at the EU level, where authorities have to come to the rescue of some member states. As already mentioned, the situation is likely to be different in "slow-burning crises" (Seabrooke and Tsingou 2019), such as the crisis linked to climate change, which does not have an initial shock that focuses everybody's attention immediately on the crisis. Given the extraordinary threat of the pandemic, the scope of the pressure it exerted on various policy domains, and its encompassing character, crisis-specific policymaking in the COVID-19 crisis is most likely to have been much more salient than in the refugee crisis at both levels of the EU polity (H1a).

During the crisis, the pressure and, therefore, the salience of policymaking will likely decrease. Following Schmidt (2022: 981), we can make a distinction between the early "fast-burning" phase and later, more "slow-burning" phases of potential normalization, when the crisis, although not resolved, no longer threatens to explode just then. With the passage of the early fast-moving phase, the salience of policymaking will likely decrease during both crises. As a result of reducing problem pressure and political pressure, the crisis in general and crisis-specific policymaking is likely to become less salient (H1b). This effect is expected to play out at both levels of the EU polity but above all at the EU level. At the national level, it may be counteracted by the attempts of political entrepreneurs to use the crisis for their purposes in later phases of the crisis when the external pressure has decreased. In the COVID-19 crisis, the diminishing salience effect will also be counteracted by the additional waves during the pandemic, likely to have kept the pressure on the policymakers.

Given that the effect of problem pressure on policymaking is mediated by political pressure (Figure 2), its direct impact on policymaking is expected to be relatively weak. Moreover, the effect of problem pressure on policymaking salience may be limited since high problem pressure may elicit rapid policy responses that are adopted without much debate – the policy responses of the ECB during the COVID-19 crisis are a case in point. By contrast, the effect of political pressure on the salience of policymaking is expected to be direct and robust (H1c). As mentioned in the previous section, this effect may also be due to the mobilization by policy entrepreneurs (H1f).

At both levels, the impact of the problem and political pressure may vary according to the policy domain in interaction with the characteristics of the policy-specific institutional context (H1d). Such policy-specific effects are most likely in the multifaceted COVID-19 crisis. At the EU level, given the EU's greater competence in economic policy, policymaking is expected to have been particularly salient in this domain, as compared to public health policy. At the national level, by contrast, lockdowns, border closures, and public health policies were arguably most directly induced by external pressure. I expect the most direct effect of external pressure on lockdowns, border closures, and public health policies. Other policy measures are likely to have followed with some time lags. In the COVID-19 crisis, where all member states were hit similarly and where policy diffusion processes occurred between member states, country-specific effects are less likely than in the refugee crisis, where the transit and open destination states experienced much greater pressure of both types during the peak of the crisis than the frontier and closed destination states (H1g).

Centrality of Actors

In addition to the overall salience of policymaking, the crisis situation also affects the relative salience of various actor types, i.e., the centrality of their role in crisis policymaking. Most generally, I expect executive decision-making to play a vital role in all crises (H2). At the level of national policymaking, even in routine politics, the transfer of power from the legislatures to the executive has been going on for a long time: The national public administration has been politicized, i.e., it has increasingly participated in the representation of interests by its involvement in the preparation of legislation and in the implementation of framework laws which left it a considerable measure of autonomy (e.g., Aberbach et al. 1981). Moreover, there have been tendencies of "executive aggrandizement," i.e., weakening checks and balances to assure executive accountability (Bermeo 2016). In the EU, such tendencies to executive decision-making have been reinforced by the increasing importance of intergovernmental decision-making, as stressed by the new intergovernmentalism (Bickerton, Hodson, and Puetter 2015; Fabbrini 2019; van Middelaar 2019). In this decision-making mode, it is the heads of member state governments (in the European Council) and responsible ministers (in the Council of the EU), including their administrative staff, who assume a decisive role, i.e., precisely those actors who have already been reinforced at the level of national policymaking.

Under crisis conditions, executive decision-making is generally expected to be reinforced to an even greater extent (for the COVID-19 crisis, see Bolleyer and Salát 2021). In a crisis situation, policymaking can no longer be confined to the policy-specific subsystem (asylum, public health, or economic policy in our case) but becomes the object of macro-politics or "Chefsache," to be taken over by the political leaders who focus on the issue in question. This claim contrasts with the claim that a critical feature of emergency politics is the emphasis on technocracy, "efficient knowledge-based rule" (White 2020: 107). In the terminology of the punctuated equilibrium model of policymaking, executive bargaining occurs due to "serial shifts" from parallel to serial processing (Baumgartner and Jones 2002). The greater the threat exerted by the crisis, the more critical the role of the government and its chief executives. Moreover, I expect the governments and top executives to play a vital role in both crises, but to a decreasing extent in later, normalizing phases of the crises, when some of the pressure has been taken off by earlier measures to deal with them and when implementation of policy decisions is more critical (H2b). Regional and local executives will likely play a more significant role in the implementation phase.

However, executive decision-making is expected to vary by crisis and polity level. At the EU level, crisis-specific conflicts are mainly intergovernmental conflicts managed by EU executives and by executives of member state governments. At the national level, by contrast, crisis-specific conflicts are often partisan, for the management of which government executives play a less critical role. As a result of these differences in the conflict management between the two levels, I expect executive decision-making to be more central at the EU level in the more conflictual refugee crisis and to be of greater centrality at the national level in the less conflictual COVID-19 crisis (H2a).

At the EU level, given the wide variation in the competence distribution in the two crises, I expect to find considerable differences in the respective roles of *EU institutions and member states*. In policy domains where the EU has high competence, EU authorities and chief executives are more likely to play an autonomous and central role in crisis resolution than in policy domains where the EU has low competence (H2d). Accordingly, I expect the EU authorities to lead in the domain of economic policy during the COVID-19 crisis. In contrast, their role is expected to have been much more limited in the public health domain during the same crisis and somewhere between during the refugee crisis.

The role of the various *transnational coalitions* is also expected to vary by crisis and policy. I show in some detail how specific coalitions shaped policy-making processes in different ways at the EU level during the two crises. However, I also expect continuity since coalitions that emerged in previous crises (solidarity coalition and Frugal 4 in the Euro Area crisis, V4 in the refugee crisis) are likely to consolidate and play a role in subsequent crises (COVID-19 crisis), too. In other words, the poly-crisis will likely have shaped a transnational configuration of coalitions that continues to structure policy-making in subsequent crises. As for variation, most importantly, in the COVID-19 crisis, the German–French coalition assumed its leadership role, while this was not the case in the refugee crisis (H2e). In the refugee crisis, Germany was largely left alone by France and had to fend for itself, supported by the supranational authorities but heavily challenged by the V4 coalition (Kriesi et al. 2024). In the COVID-19 crisis, by contrast, Germany's dependence on maintaining its export markets (Schramm 2023) and the fact that France, as part of the solidarity coalition, was driving for joint solutions motivated renewed leadership by the German–French coalition. Moreover, two contingent factors enhanced Germany's role in managing the COVID-19 crisis. On the one hand, at the decisive European Council meeting in July 2020, Germany occupied the role of the rotating Presidency, which allowed it to assume a dominant role in the negotiations of the RRF (Schelkle 2021: 53). On the other hand, in dealing with the COVID-19 crisis, the key decision-makers, especially the German ones, were able and ready to build on their experiences with earlier crises (Quaglia and Verdun 2023). During the COVID-19 crisis, Germany's change of mind in the case of the RRF and vaccination procurement can probably also be attributed to the fact that it was led by the most seasoned European politician – Angela Merkel, who had already been a critical decision-maker in the previous crises, and who had arrived in the twilight of her long career at the time she was to preside over the RRF negotiations (Ferrera, Miró, and Ronchi 2021).

At the national level, the crisis situation reinforced the role of *EU-polity actors* and *political parties* in the refugee crisis, both of whom mobilized opposition against government proposals. In contrast, three other types of actors are likely to have played a more critical role in the COVID-19 crisis: *local and regional governments, civil society organizations* (*including business actors*), and *experts* (H2f). Local and regional governments have been influential in the COVID-19 crisis because they are typically responsible for implementing public health policies in European countries. As far as experts are concerned, faced with great uncertainty, policymakers sought the advice of medical experts (virologists, epidemiologists, public health experts) who became essential participants in the process (Lavazza and Farina 2020). A study of their role in the Swiss government's policymaking shows, however, that their role diminished throughout the pandemic because their advice was increasingly questioned by parties and interest associations (Eichenberger et al. 2023). Interest groups, in turn, got increasing access to decision-makers to the extent that the interests they represented were affected by the crisis, primarily if they represented economic interests (Junk et al. 2022).

These general expectations need to be qualified in at least one respect: The precise role played by a given type of actor also depends on country-specific circumstances, which include institutional factors (e.g., federal vs unitary states), government composition (e.g., one-party vs coalition governments), and party strategies (e.g., responsive vs responsible strategy) (H2g). Thus, in a federal state, local and regional authorities play a more significant role in policymaking than in a unitary state, especially in policy implementation, which was crucial in the COVID-19 crisis. Second, when an anti-EU party is in government, as was the case in Hungary, where Viktor Orbán has governed since 2010, or in the case of Italy, where a populist, anti-EU coalition came to power in the summer of 2018 and governed for roughly one year, the role of partisan opposition to EU proposals may be played by the government itself, which serves to enhance the role of the government and reduce the role of parties in the policy debate (since parties in government were coded as government actors). Third, the government's party composition is also essential because coalition governments are often internally divided about the policy to be adopted, increasing their prominence during the policy debates.

Support of Government Proposals

Schattschneider (1975: 3) has taught us the importance of the expansion of the scope of conflict: "So great is the change of any conflict likely to be as a consequence of the widening involvement of people in it that the original participants are apt to lose control of the conflict altogether." Applied to our conceptual scheme, we generally expect that the extent of support for government proposals depends on the extent to which executive actors prevail (H3). The more the executive actors of the government remain in control of the policymaking process, the greater the likelihood that the proposal is supported. To the extent that additional participants come in, i.e., as the scope of conflict expands, policy support is expected to decrease. At least this should apply at the national level. At the EU level, there is one caveat: Executive actors generally prevail, but they are the main antagonists in intergovernmental policymaking.

This means that, in case of conflict, they will not be able to control the process precisely because they remain among themselves.

Given the unprecedented and existential character of the COVID-19 crisis, the greater symmetry of its incidence, its more limited politicization by parties, and the corresponding greater control by executive actors at the national level, this crisis is expected to be much more consensual than the refugee crisis at both levels of the EU polity (H3a). More specifically, I expect this difference to apply to the early phases of the COVID-19 crisis, when the government will likely have benefited from a rallying effect (H3b). It is well known that under exceptional circumstances, the *public* tends to line up behind the government, resulting in what Mueller (1970) coined as the "rally around the flag" effect: a short-term boost to political leaders' popularity or job approval. For the COVID-19 crisis, a rallying effect has already been documented by a series of studies (Altiparmakis et al. 2021; Baekgaard et al. 2020; Bol et al. 2021; Esaiasson et al. 2021; Schraff 2021; van der Meer, Steenvoorden, and Ouattara 2023). I argue that such an effect also operates at the policymaking level: *Policymakers* in the policy domain in question rally behind the government in an attempt to come to terms with the extraordinary crisis situation. The tremendous pressure at the origin of the crisis creates a sense of purpose and urgency that induces all policymakers to agree to the immediate response proposed by the government, i.e., urgency can be a productive force (Birkland 2009). Policymakers need to act very quickly to contain the scope and scale of the disaster and they may agree under the functional pressure of the "normative power of the facts." As the virus struck again in a second and third wave, similar "rallying" effects may even occur in later phases of the crisis, i.e., I expect problem and political pressure to increase policy support throughout the COVID-19 crisis (H3c).

By contrast, the refugee crisis intervened in a policy domain that had already been highly politicized before the crisis and which provided a unique opportunity for the radical right and its followers to mobilize opposition to the government and its emergency measures in terms of identity, all of which serve to undermine a rallying effect, again at both levels of the EU polity. In this crisis, increasing external pressure is expected to contribute to politicizing the crisis, which does not improve the support for the government's policies. By contributing to the politicization of the crisis, increasing problem and political pressure may even undermine the support for government policies in the case of the refugee crisis.

In the EU polity, the member states are the critical actors for joint solutions at the EU level since the EU authorities tend to favor such solutions by default. The relative autonomy and centrality of supranational actors and fellow member state governments may be constrained or facilitated by *transnational coalitions* between member states. Especially in a policy domain such as asylum policy, where sovereigntist-identitarian principles play a crucial role, I expect the mobilization of adversarial transnational coalitions to undermine joint solutions at the EU level (H3e). Moreover, in the refugee crisis, such conflicts are expected to spill over into national policymaking, where they are exacerbated by partisan conflicts that mobilize national identities, reinforcing transnational disputes. Conversely, in this crisis, national conflicts are likely to spill over to the transnational level because of the externalities created by the unilateral actions of member states for other member states. By contrast, in the COVID-19 crisis, such spillovers across polity levels are unlikely to occur. The EU did not attempt to intervene actively in the policymaking process of its member states, nor did member states try to upload their problems to the EU level (Truchlewski et al. 2023). Moreover, there were hardly any policy externalities between member states, which they could mutually blame on each other. In the COVID-19 crisis, as already mentioned, national and EU-polity conflict structures remained essentially *segmented* as a by-product of the crisis situation and the unstructured partisan conflicts at the national level.

As I have observed in the section on political pressure, domestically, the governments of member states come under pressure from two sides – the EU polity (transnational coalitions and supranational actors) and domestic opposition. In the refugee crisis, I expect EU-polity actors to have been particularly critical of national governments, especially regarding frontline states, whose unilateral policies created significant externalities for the other member states. Domestically, the government faces multiple potential adversaries in all crises: opposition parties, civil society (including experts), and the local and regional authorities. As we have seen, in the case of Germany, opposition even came from governing parties and from within the cabinet during the refugee crisis. Given the consensual character of the COVID-19 crisis, I expect all domestic actors, including the opposition parties and civil society actors who tend to be particularly critical, to provide more support for the government than in the refugee crisis (H3f). However, in their competition with the government parties, opposition parties can be expected to exploit the crisis situation and attack the government for doing too much or too little in its crisis management, even in a relatively consensual crisis like the COVID-19 crisis. Critical civil society organizations are crisis-specific but can also be expected to oppose government policy proposals independently of the type of crisis. Given their generally adversarial outlook, these two actor types are likely to be of critical importance for the rallying effect as they have a lot of maneuvering room to improve their government support (see Louwerse et al. (2021) for opposition parties during the COVID-19 crisis).

These expectations need again to be qualified in at least one respect: The precise support by a given type of actor depends on country-specific circumstances – on institutional aspects (e.g., the government's composition or its administrative capacity) and strategic elements (e.g., strategies of opposition parties), and it may vary by policy domain in a given crisis, depending on the popularity of the proposed policies in the national general public (H3g).

Policy Output

The fourth dependent variable refers to policy output. First, one might expect a close link between policy support and policy output: Policy support is generally likely to facilitate policy output (H4). Accordingly, given that the authorities' proposals will have received more significant support at both levels during the COVID-19 than during the refugee crisis, we can expect greater substantive policy output at both levels in the former than in the latter (H4a). In the later phases of both crises, we expect policy output to decline (H4b) due to the policy output already adopted during the early phases of a crisis, which is likely to diminish the functional and political pressure. However, to the extent that this pressure keeps up, we expect it to continue facilitating policy responses. External pressure will likely induce policymakers to develop policy responses (H4c).

The link between policy support and policy output may seem obvious. Still, under tremendous pressure during a crisis, policy support may be less relevant than one tends to assume at first sight. Exogenous pressure may force executive policymakers to come up with a response, even if broad sections of the political elite do not support them. Tremendous pressure may lead to a rallying effect, facilitating policy responses to the crisis. However, to the extent that policymakers are not rallying around the government's proposals, the decision-makers may ignore their resistance because they need to respond to the pressure. Problem and political pressure enhance the authorities' policy response, even against the opposition of essential participants in the policymaking process. This effect is expected to apply to the COVID-19 crisis in particular. Given the existential character of the COVID-19 crisis and its overall less politicized character, the exogenous pressure is likely to allow executive decision-makers to push through policy responses even against resistance (H4f). In the case of the more conflictual context of the refugee crisis, however, pressure is likely to increase politicization, as I have argued in the section on political pressure, which means that support for the authorities' policymaking is more challenging to achieve: Lacking the required support for the policy response, the latter is unlikely to be forthcoming.

At the EU level, adversarial coalitions may block joint solutions, while supportive coalitions may enhance the coordination capacity of supranational actors even in policy domains where they have little competence. Given the high threshold of consensus requirements in EU intergovernmental decision-making, *transnational coalitions* can obtain disproportional power at the EU level. Especially in a policy domain where sovereigntist-identitarian principles play a crucial role, such as asylum policy, the intransigence of such a coalition can block EU policymaking decisively, even if unanimity is not required (H4e). As I have argued in the section on policy-specific institutional context, the German–French coalition assumed a leadership role in the COVID-19 crisis, facilitating the EU's crisis management. It played no such role in the refugee crisis, which negatively affected the EU's capacity for crisis management. It is likely that Germany's limited capacity to play, on its own, the role of a stabilizing hegemonic power in the EU during the refugee crisis has been crucial for the inability of the EU to find stable solutions to this crisis (Webber 2019: 17).

In addition to the overall pressure, country-specific conditions, such as the administrative capacities (Popic and Moise 2022; Toshkov, Carroll, and Yesilkagit 2022), diffusion processes (Sebhatu et al. 2020), a combination of psychological, institutional, and strategic factors (Maor and Howlett 2020) or the member state type (during the refugee crisis) may also influence the government's response (H4g).

Conclusion

Table 1 summarizes the hypotheses which will guide the analysis. Most hypotheses expect differences between the two crises. The exceptions concern the great salience of crisis-specific policymaking, especially at the origin of the crisis, executive decision-making, and the EU's more significant role in crisis policymaking in general. In addition, we may generally expect diminishing effects on the various aspects of policymaking in the later phases of both crises. The critical differences between policymaking in the two crises concern three factors: I expect policymaking to have been more salient, supported, and successful in the COVID-19 crisis than in the refugee crisis. I expect greater contentiousness in the refugee crisis due to the absence of joint German–French leadership, the presence of adversarial transnational coalitions at the EU level, cross-level spillovers, and the combined opposition by EU-polity actors and domestic political parties at the national level. As a result of the greater contentiousness of the refugee crisis, at both levels of the EU polity, I expect a rallying effect for the

Table 1 Summary of hypotheses[a]

Dimension	Salience	Centrality	Support	Output
crisis policy-making, in general	**H1**: high salience of crisis policy-making, especially at the EU level	**H2**: executive decision-making prevails	**H3**: executive decision-making increases support	**H4**: support facilitates substantive solutions
crisis-specific in general	**H1a**: salience: *cov>ref*	**H2a**: executive decision-making: EU: *ref>cov*; ms: *cov>ref*	**H3a**: support: *cov>ref*	**H4a**: *cov*: greater support induces more policy out-put than in *ref*
phase-specific	**H1b**: diminishing salience in later waves, especially at the EU level	**H2b**: diminishing role of executive decision-making in later waves	**H3b**: rallying effect: *cov>ref*	**H4b**: diminishing policy output in later waves
pressure-specific	**H1c**: weak direct effect of problem pressure/strong effect of political pressure on salience in *cov&ref*		**H3c**: problem/political pressure increases support in *cov*, but not in *ref*	**H4c**: problem/political pressure facilitates response in *cov*, but not in *ref*
policy-specific: EU *vs* MS	**H1d**: *cov*: EU: focus on economic policy ms: focus on lockdown, public health	**H2d**: EU role: economic>asylum> public health		

Table 1 (cont.)

Dimension	Salience	Centrality	Support	Output
actor-specific, transnational coalitions		**H2e:** EU level: *cov:* governments less central and more limited role of transnational conflicts	**H3e:** *ref:* greater resistance by transnational coalitions/more cross-level spillover effects	**H4e:** *cov:* German-French leadership vs. *ref:* blocking capacity of hostile coalitions
actor-specific, domestic level	**H1f:** salience induced by policy entrepreneurs	**H2f:** *ref:* greater role of – actors/parties vs *cov:* greater role of regional-local/ experts/cs	**H3f:** All non-executive actors are less supportive in *ref* than in *cov*	**H4f:** *cov:* executive actors push through policy responses against resistance
country-specific	**H1g:** country-specific effects in *ref*, but not in *cov*	**H2g:** country-specific context	**H3g:** country-specific context	**H4g:** country-specific context

ª cov = COVID-19 crisis, ref = refugee crisis; EU = EU level, ms = member state; cs = civil society; > = bigger than

COVID-19 crisis, but not for the refugee crisis; I expect pressure to facilitate the policy response at both levels in the former, but not in the latter; and I expect blocked joint solutions at the EU level in the refugee crisis, which leads to stop-gap, second-best solutions. In contrast, sustainable collaborative solutions are expected to be much more likely in the COVID-19 crisis. Policy-specific and country-specific modifications complete these expectations. Thus, the competence distribution in the EU polity and country-specific factors alone or in combination are expected to modify the role of the EU in policy-specific ways.

3 Design

General Methodological Approach

For the empirical analysis of the policymaking processes, I rely on policy process analysis (PPA) (Bojar et al. 2023), a comprehensive method for the data collection and analysis of policymaking debates. Policymaking has a core of puzzling and powering, which occurs in specific and not always transparent arenas. Yet, it also gives rise to many external signals reaching the public sphere, primarily through the mass media. Policy process analysis intends to capture this public face of policymaking. In its design, PPA draws upon protest event analysis (PEA) (Hutter 2014), contentious episode analysis (Bojar et al. 2023), and political claims analysis (Koopmans and Statham 1999) but broadens its focus beyond contention to policymaking debates more generally. Similar to these other methods, PPA is an event-based methodology that focuses on identifying distinct *policy actions* in the media, undertaken by various *actors*, addressing particular *issues*, and how they unfold over time concerning the core of the policymaking process. Policy process analysis is also related to the Comparative Policy Agendas approach (Baumgartner, Green-Pedersen, and Jones 2006). However, it goes beyond it because PPA is not limited to the agenda-setting phase but includes all significant steps in the policymaking process, from agenda-setting to implementation. The PPA data provides the essential characteristics of the policymaking process.

For the systematic analysis of the effects of the crisis situation on policymaking, the PPA data is aggregated and combined with data on the crisis situation and on policy output taken from various existing sources to create a dataset where the episode-month (refugee crisis) or the country-week (COVID-19 crisis) constitutes the units of analysis. I now detail the different steps in constructing the two basic types of datasets and the procedures to analyze this data.

Selection of the Period

Given the protracted period of the refugee crisis and the more intermittent policymaking process during this crisis, the SOLID project team[4] decided to break it down into a set of crucial policymaking *episodes*, which salient policy proposals have triggered. Some of the policies the team has chosen are legislative acts, such as reforms to the countries' asylum systems; others are administrative decisions and novel practices by state institutions, such as the reimposition of border controls in a heightened period of problem pressure. A policy episode comprises the entire policy debate surrounding these specific policy proposals that governments put forward, from when the proposal enters the public debate to when it is implemented and the discussion surrounding it is no longer salient. The episodes cover the period from the beginning of 2013 until the end of February 2020. There are forty-six policymaking episodes (six EU-level episodes and five episodes each for eight countries), which were spread over the pre-peak period (January 2013–July 2015), the peak period (August 2015–March 2016), which ended with the adoption of the EU–Turkey agreement, and the long-tailed post-peak period (April 2016–February 2020). For the present analysis, I focus on the peak period (first wave) and the post-peak period (second wave) and exclude the two pre-peak episodes (one from Italy and one from the UK) from the analysis.

For the COVID-19 crisis, the team adopted a different procedure because the policymaking processes were not coded retrospectively but in real time, which means it would have been hard to identify policymaking episodes in advance. The team coded all policy actions (irrespective of policy domain) identified in the national press and related to COVID-19 from March 2020 to December 2021. Based on the epidemiological development of the crisis, this period is split into three waves: first wave (March 2020–August 2020), second wave (September 2020–May 2021), and third wave (June 2021–December 2021). For specific analyses, the second and third waves are often combined.

Selection of the Countries

For the refugee crisis, the team selected eight countries: two transit states (Austria and Hungary), two open destination states (Germany and Sweden), two frontier states (Greece and Italy), and two closed destination states (France

---

[4] The policy processes of the two crises were coded in the framework of the SOLID project, an ERC-Synergy project located at the European University Institute, at the University of Milano, and (originally) at the London School of Economics. The EUI team mainly operated the coding for the two crises.

and the UK).[5] Figure 3 presents the development of problem pressure and political pressure for the selected countries. For the refugee crisis, problem pressure is measured by the monthly submissions of asylum requests as a percentage of the population; political pressure is measured as public salience by Google Trends data.[6] As can be seen from Figure 3a, the two transit states (Austria and Hungary) and the two open destination states (Germany and Sweden) took a hit immediately in the fall of 2015, while the two frontier states (Greece and Italy) and the two closed destination states (France and UK) were initially not confronted with a similar challenge. The Mediterranean frontier states were also directly concerned by the inflow of refugees because, under prevailing EU law and the Dublin regulation, they were responsible for registering and accommodating the incoming refugees. Initially, however, they were spared more severe consequences because of the secondary movements of refugees to other member states. Once these secondary movements were stopped by adopting the EU–Turkey agreement in March 2016, Greece, but not Italy, received more asylum requests, too.

As the figure shows for the refugee crisis, in the transit and open destination states, i.e., in the states most exposed to the secondary movements, *public salience* peaked with problem pressure early on in the crisis. After the initial peak, both problem pressure and public salience dropped in these countries. In the frontier states, by contrast, we observe multiple peaks of public salience. In Greece, it peaked twice, at the moment of the exogenous shock and then again at the end of the period covered by the crisis, due to internal conflicts on the islands and external pressure from Turkish President Erdogan (see Kriesi et al. 2024: 291–93).

In Italy, public salience even peaked three times: pre-crisis, i.e., during the Mare Nostrum rescue operation, which was launched by Italy after an awful shipwreck in the fall of 2013, at the moment of shock in the fall of 2015, and then again in the summer and fall of 2018, when the Minister of the Interior of the new populist coalition government, Matteo Salvini, used the rescue operations of NGOs in the Mediterranean to mobilize public opinion against refugees. However, public opinion was flatlined in the two closed destination states, although a peak of public salience was also visible at the peak of the crisis in the UK.

For the COVID-19 crisis, we covered ten countries representative of the various transnational coalitions that shaped up during the first wave of this crisis: the German–French coalition, three members of the Frugal 4 (Austria, the Netherlands, and Sweden), the UK (still a member during the first two waves),

---

[5] For more details on the distinction between these four types of member states in the refugee crisis of 2015–16, see Kriesi et al. (2021) and Kriesi et al. (2024).

[6] To gather the Google Trends data for the refugee crisis, we analyzed the salience in Google searches of the following topics and search terms: Immigration – Topic and Refugee – Search Term.

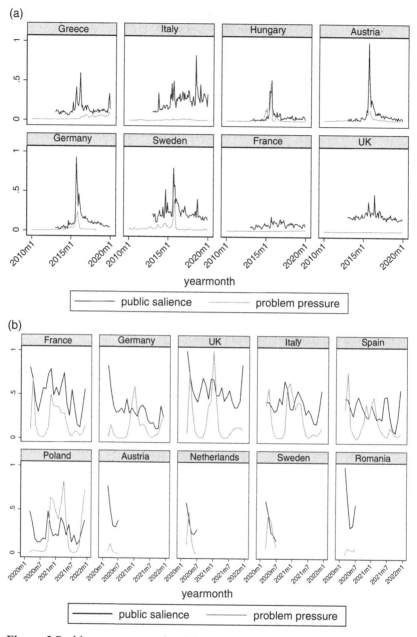

Figure 3 Problem pressure and political pressure by crisis, country, and time. Problem pressure: monthly submissions of asylum requests as a percentage of the population for the refugee crisis and new monthly deaths for the COVID-19 crisis; political pressure: public salience as indicated by Google Trends. For gathering the Google Trends data, we analyzed the salience in Google searches of the following topics and search terms: Immigration – Topic and Refugee – Search Term for the refugee crisis; coronavirus – Topic, Covid, COVID-19- Search Terms for the COVID-19 crisis. For four countries during the COVID-19 crisis, information is only available for the first period.

two Southern European (Italy and Spain), and two Eastern European countries (Poland and Romania). For the later waves, we focused on the six largest: Germany, France, Spain, Italy, Poland, and the UK. Four countries have been included throughout both crises (Germany, France, Italy, and the UK) and can be relied upon for more focused comparisons.

For the COVID-19 crisis, I use the number of monthly new deaths to indicate problem pressure.[7] Google Trends data measure political pressure once again. This crisis developed in three waves, as can be seen (see Figure 3b) for the six countries (France, Germany, UK, Italy, Spain, and Poland) for which we have detailed information for all three waves. The timing of the crisis varied, however, by region. The crisis spared Eastern Europe (Poland) in the first wave but hit it all the harder in the third wave, while Southern (Italy and Spain) and Northwestern (France, Germany, UK) Europe were equally hit early on and in the second wave (in fall 2020). The four additional countries (Austria, the Netherlands, Sweden, and Romania), for which we have detailed data on the first wave only, confirm the timing effect: Western European countries all experienced the early shock, although Austria (and Germany) less so than others, while Romania, just as Poland, was spared by it. In economic terms, all countries were hit by the COVID-19 crisis, but Western Europe, especially Southern Europe, fared less well than Eastern Europe. In sum, if the problem pressure in the COVID-19 crisis was more symmetrical than in the refugee crisis, it still varied in timing and the extent of its incidence across countries.

Public salience was generally not closely aligned with problem pressure in the COVID-19 crisis. It peaked in all the countries right at the beginning of the crisis, when the exogenous shock hit. Still, after this initial peak, it oscillated heavily throughout the crisis, reaching similar peaks again during later waves in all countries except Germany, where it declined after the initial shock.

Policy Process Analysis

Having set the scope of our data collection, the first step in constructing the PPA dataset is defining and gathering the media corpus to be analyzed (Bojar et al. 2023). Depending on the level of policymaking, the SOLID team selected either international news sources (for the EU level) or, respectively, national news sources (for the level of the member states). The team used the news aggregator platform Factiva for document retrieval. This platform provided access to many media outlets, allowing for systematic multicountry comparison and transparent

---

[7] The number of monthly new cases would be an alternative indicator. Still, it has the disadvantage that it does not indicate a threat to the same extent throughout the crisis: Once the vaccination was introduced in 2021, the strongly rising number of cases was no longer as threatening as they were initially.

and replicable selection criteria on the source. Following good practice in working with media data from methods such as protest event analysis (Hutter 2014), the team also tried to engage with issues of *selection bias* (e.g., Earl et al. 2004; Ortiz et al. 2006), that is, with the biases associated with news source selection and their coverage of debates, actions, or events. To mitigate such biases, the team adopted several strategies. First, it relied on various media sources, rather than a single source, to capture as many aspects of the policy debates as possible. Second, to mitigate biases related to newsworthiness and proximity, the team selected news sources that are proximate to the level of analysis: For EU debates, it focused on large news agencies and the international press (Agence France Presse, the Associated Press, Reuters, Financial Times, Euronews, ANSA, BBC, MTI), while for national debates it relied on national media. Third, to mitigate biases related to the political motives of the various sources and their potential impact on news coverage, the team selected news sources from different sides of the political spectrum. Consequently, for each country, the team aimed to choose one major newspaper left of center and one right of center regarding ideological leaning (with some minor exceptions related to data availability).

After selecting the news sources, the second decision related to corpus construction consisted in identifying the keywords used to retrieve articles. At this step, one of the primary considerations is achieving a balanced relevance ratio – the ratio between false positives (irrelevant articles that the keyword combination retrieved as positive hits) and false negatives (relevant articles that the keyword combination filtered out as negative hits). Since the data is manually coded, the team aimed for a relatively slim but robust corpus. That is, the corpus ought to be manageable in terms of the number of articles identified in order not to make the coding process too cumbersome and resource-intensive but should still allow capturing the full range of actions in a given country without missing relevant articles filtered out by a too restrictive keyword combination. In practical terms, the selection of keywords was performed by team members in close collaboration with a team of native-language-speaking coders (mostly comprised of political science Ph.D. students also knowledgeable about the subject at hand).[8] At this stage, the team took

---

[8] For the COVID-19 crisis, the keyword selection consisted of translated versions of the following string: (coronavirus or covid) and (law* or measure* or decree* or decision*) and (European Union*), where the European Union was replaced with member state names for the coding of policy actions at the member state level. For the refugee crisis, the team constructed more complex search strings. For each episode, it chose an initial set of episode-specific keywords based on secondary sources (policy reports, secondary scientific literature, etc.) and initial search queries in the national press. It then further refined this initial keyword selection through an iterative process of going back and forth between the selection and the corpus obtained. The team selected those keyword combinations that passed the initial reading of the selected articles and achieved a satisfactory balance between the size of the corpus and the number of events filtered out.

advantage of the capabilities of the news aggregator Factiva, which allowed us to construct complex search strings using Boolean algebra and its standard logical operators.

After constructing the corpus, the last step in the PPA coding process consists of action coding. As already mentioned, PPA is an event-based methodology; hence, the observation unit at the level at which the data is collected is an action, i.e., "an act or a claim by an actor with a prominent role in the political world that has a direct or indirect relevance for the policy debate" (Bojar et al. 2023). Therefore, actions can be steps in the policymaking process, verbal claims, or protest events within our framework. To measure the various features of actions, action coding is based on a common core of variables that are coded for each of the actions: the arena where the action takes place, its (procedural) form, its (substantive) type of engagement with the policy, its overall direction vis-a-vis the policy, its direction vis-a-vis target actors, the organizational characteristics of the actor undertaking the action and of the target actors, the issues it engages with, and the normative frames used by actors to present their positions to the public (Bojar et al. 2023). Note that while the lowest level of observation is an action, the unit of analysis can be pitched at any level of aggregation (actor types, issue categories, types of countries, etc.) as needed for the analysis.

Datasets

Overall, the corpus for the comparison includes 28,926 policy actions. Roughly, three-fourths relate to the COVID-19 crisis (21,245), and one-fourth (7,681) to the refugee crisis. Most of the actions (84 percent) in each crisis refer to the national level, roughly one-sixth of which are at the EU level. The distribution of the coded actions confirms the unique salience of the COVID-19 crisis, although it is also partly a result of the different procedures applied in the two crises. This corpus constitutes the basic "action file."

Based on this file, I constructed two additional files for national-level analyses, one each for the two crises, including PPA data and context data for the two types of pressure and the policy output. I have already introduced the indicators used for the problem and political pressure in the previous section – monthly submissions of asylum requests as a percentage of the population for problem pressure in the refugee crisis, and new weekly deaths for problem pressure during the COVID-19 crisis, as well as monthly and weekly Google trends for political pressure in both crises. For policy output, systematic measures are only available for the COVID-19 crisis. There are three indicators: a general indicator for the government's response, an indicator for the stringency of the government's lockdown measures, and one for the economic response.[9] For the analysis, I recoded the corresponding indicators, like all the other independent variables, to the 0–1 range, which means that the results will show the maximum effects for each variable.

The unit of analysis in these additional files is the episode-month for the refugee crisis and the country-week for the COVID-19 crisis. I chose monthly units for the refugee crisis because, in this case, data on problem and political pressure are, at best, available every month. A more fine-grained analysis would also not have been possible because of the scarcity of the PPA data during the refugee crisis. We would have ended up with many units with no actions at all had we relied on weekly data. For the COVID-19 crisis, it is possible to use weekly data because all the context variables are available every week, and the PPA data are sufficiently rich for analyses by weeks. I use both a wide and a long form of this dataset. In the wide format, the unit of analysis is the country-week combination, and the PPA indicators are coded by policy domain. In the long version, there is a country-week combination for each policy domain, of which there are six in this crisis (see the next section). Overall, the episode-month file for the refugee crisis includes 551 units, with the number of units per month in the individual episodes varying from a minimum of 4 to a maximum of 34. The country-week file in the wide format for the COVID-19 crisis includes 96 weeks for the six countries we covered in all three waves, i.e., 574 country-weeks and 21 weeks for the four countries covered only in the first wave.

Operationalization of Key Dependent Variables

Previous analyses of policymaking based on PPA data (e.g., Bojar and Kriesi 2023) have mainly relied on indicators for politicization and its components (salience and polarization). I primarily rely on three indicators for the present analysis: salience, centrality, and support. The *salience* is a system-level property measured by the absolute number of policymaking actions in a given crisis, wave, or policy. Although it is hard to compare across crises because of the different approaches used to collect the data, salience still provides a rough idea of the order of magnitude of the extent to which a crisis dominated the policy-making process at a given time. For most analyses, I recoded the salience indicator per crisis to the 0–1 range. When focusing on the actors' role in the policymaking process, it is more appropriate to measure the *centrality* of the actor, i.e., the *relative* salience of an actor in such a process, which corresponds to the share of all the policy actions in a given policymaking process for which the actor is responsible. I do not use the concept of polarization in the present analysis because it is primarily a system-level property. Instead, I replace it with

---

[9] These indicators are taken from the Oxford COVID-19 Government Response Tracker OxCGRT.

the concept of *support*, which has the advantage that it is easily applied to both the system level and to individual actors. It corresponds to the average direction of the policy-specific positions taken by the actors in a crisis, a wave, or a policy domain at a given level, measured on a scale ranging from −1 (complete opposition to) to +1 (full support of) the policy proposal. For *policy output*, we only have the three indicators already introduced at the national level in the COVID-19 crisis. Otherwise, we have to rely on qualitative information.

I recoded the multiple issues into a limited set of crisis-specific policy domains, as shown in Table 2. For the COVID-19 crisis, I distinguish between six policy domains – economic, fiscal, lockdowns (restrictions and relaxations), public health, vaccination, and institutional questions (questions mainly concerning emergency powers, rules of civil liberties, suspension of institutional procedures such as parliamentary sessions, or postponement of elections). At the EU level, economic policies mainly refer to single market policies, while fiscal policies mainly concern the RRF. As shown in (a) in Table 2, in the COVID-19 crisis, economic and fiscal policies and vaccination policies predominate at the EU level, while financial, public health, and lockdown-border closure measures prevail at the national level. For the refugee crisis, we can distinguish between border closures and asylum-integration policies, which include the bulk of policymaking at the national level and the three most important EU-specific policy episodes (EU–Turkey agreement, relocation scheme, and Dublin reform).

Data Analysis

The data analysis mainly relies on straightforward descriptive tools, ranging from bar charts to OLS regressions. The independent variables include the type of crisis (COVID-19 vs refugee crisis), the polity level, the period (first to third waves), country, problem and political pressure, actor type, and policy domain. The basic actor typology distinguishes between eight types: EU-polity actors, governments, governing and opposition parties, local–regional authorities, experts, and civil society. EU-polity actors include the EU Commission, other EU actors (supranational actors), and the governments of (other) member states (transnational coalitions). When not mentioned otherwise, I use the action file. For analyses, including indicators for the problem and political pressure, I rely, depending on the crisis, on the episode-month and the country-week files. Given the prevailing short series in the episode-month file for the refugee crisis, the analyses report contemporaneous effects in a given month, i.e., I do not analyze longitudinal dynamics for this crisis. Given the extended series for the six countries covered throughout the three waves, relying on more complex dynamic panel analyses for the COVID-19 crisis is possible.

Table 2 Policy domains in the two crises: percentages

(a) COVID−19 crisis

Policy Domains	National	EU	Total
Economic (single market)	21.9	14.8	15.4
Fiscal (RRF)	3.4	25.1	2.9
Vaccination	13.4	20.3	14.5
Public health	20.7	9.1	18.8
Lockdown-border closures	34.9	16.0	31.9
Institutional issues	5.8	14.6	10.2
Total	100.0	100.0	100.0
n	17,792	3,348	21,140

(b) Refugee Crisis

Policy Domains	National	EU	Total
Border control	21.3	4.5	18.6
Asylum-integration (hotspots)	65.4	11.4	56.5
EU–Turkey agreement	0.0	34.8	5.7
Relocation	0.0	26.4	4.3
Dublin	0.0	16.9	2.8
Other	13.3	6.1	12.1
Total	100.0	100.0	100.0
n	6,410	1,255	7,665

The results will be presented in three sections. The next section analyzes crisis policymaking from the perspective of salience and centrality, i.e., from the standpoint of the prominence of the overall process and the role played by specific actor types in the process. Section 5 analyzes policy support, i.e., the conflicts involved in the policymaking process and their consequences. Section 6 will focus on policy output.

4 Salience and Centrality

Salience

To begin with, I want to document the great salience of the immediate response of policymakers at both levels in the two crises, especially at the EU level (H1), the overwhelming salience of the COVID-19 crisis (H1a), and the declining salience in the course of the two crises (H1b). Figure 4 presents the average monthly salience of policy actions during the three (COVID-19) and two (refugee crisis) waves of these crises. For the member states, I calculate the

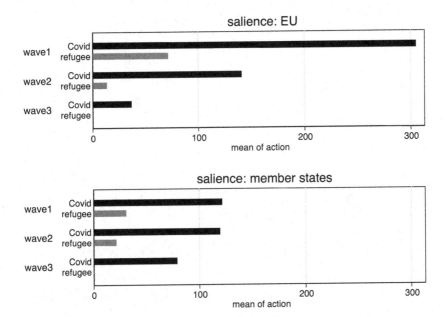

Figure 4 Salience by level, wave, and crisis: number of actions.

average across member states for which we have complete data for all waves. All expectations are confirmed. First, salience immediately surged early in the two crises (H1), especially at the EU level. EU policymaking during the first wave was much more salient than policymaking in the average member state during the same period. The results confirm that, in the EU polity, crises pose a particularly intense challenge for policymakers at the EU level: They have to come to the rescue of hard-hit member states (in asymmetric crises such as the refugee crisis) or of member states lacking the capacity to respond to the crisis (in symmetric crises such as the COVID-19 crisis) to maintain a level-playing field. They must coordinate the member states' response and build additional supranational capacity to deal with the crisis.

Second, policymaking in the COVID-19 crisis was much more salient than in the refugee crisis (H1a). Third, in both crises, the salience in later waves declines as expected (H1b). The decline is particularly noteworthy at the EU level during the refugee crisis. After adopting the EU–Turkey agreement, which concluded the first phase of the crisis, EU policymaking became much less conspicuous. In the COVID-19 crisis, salience declines at the national level only in the third wave. But even if its salience declines, national policymaking remains much more prominent than ever during the refugee crisis. The second and third waves of the pandemic kept policymaking focused on the crisis. This impact documents the extent to which Europe was in the thrall of the virus for more than a year.

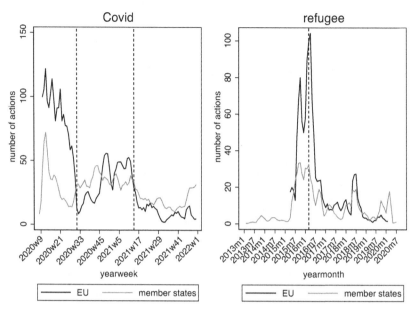

Figure 5 Time line of the salience of crisis-specific policymaking, by crisis and level: absolute weekly number of actions, smoothed.

Figure 5 provides a more detailed time line for the salience of crisis-specific policymaking. It presents three-weekly (COVID-19) and three-monthly (refugee crisis) moving averages of the number of actions.[10] The vertical lines indicate the waves in the case of the COVID-19 crisis and the adoption of the EU–Turkey agreement in the case of the refugee crisis. We observe that, in the COVID-19 crisis, policymakers reacted immediately at both levels, even more so at the EU level, as the exogenous shock hit. Policymaking activity reaches its peak almost instantly and then declines throughout the first wave of the crisis, more rapidly at the member state level than at the EU level, where the negotiations about the RRF kept policymakers busy until the end of July 2020. Policymaking resumed again during the second wave, but now it is relatively more salient in the member states. While the EU provided short-term and even long-term economic support during the first wave in line with its essential competence in this domain – roughly two-thirds of its policymaking during this wave focused on economic policies (H1d), it turned to support in vaccination during later waves – almost half of EU policymaking in wave two and roughly a third in wave 3 concerned vaccination, a policy domain, where the EU

---

[10] Note that the salience is only comparable within a crisis, but not between crises, since the time lines have different units of analysis.

had acquired new competences in the course of the crisis. During the third wave, policymaking at both levels drops off, but more so at the EU level, since the EU has now supported both policy domains of crucial concern during the COVID-19 crisis.

In the refugee crisis, there was a first attempt at crisis policymaking at both levels in the spring of 2015. But this aborts because of political resistance. When the crisis hit in earnest at the end of the summer of 2015, policymakers responded immediately at both levels, especially at the EU level. At this level, salience is double-peaked during the first wave. The two peaks correspond to the solutions proposed by EU policymakers – the relocation scheme and the EU–Turkey agreement. First, the EU focused on the relocation scheme, which was responsible for almost half of the actions during the first peak. Only when this solution failed because of the resistance of the V4 coalition did the EU home in on its plan B, the EU–Turkey agreement, which is responsible for almost two-thirds of the action during the second peak. In the long second wave of the refugee crisis, we observe a minor third peak at both levels in the summer of 2018, which corresponds to the attempt of the German Chancellor Merkel to find a solution to her domestic intraparty conflicts at the EU level, an attempt that failed ignominiously (see Kriesi et al. 2024).

As we have seen, the member states experienced *similar* ups and downs in the levels of problem and political pressure during the COVID-19 crisis but faced *different* levels of such pressure in the refugee crisis (see Figure 3): Only the transit and open destination states experienced a cumulation of both types of pressure during the peak wave of the crisis. The frontline and closed destination states were less pressured. The question is whether this difference in pressure leads to differences in the salience of policymaking (H1g). Figure 6 provides a first answer to this question. It presents the time lines of the salience of crisis-specific policymaking by type of member state in the refugee crisis. As expected, policymaking picked up in response to the external shock in the transit and open destination states in the summer of 2015, and it decreased in these countries once the problem pressure was somewhat constrained after adopting the EU–Turkey agreement. However, during this peak period, policy-making also increased in the frontline and closed destination states, which have hardly been exposed to problem pressure (as measured by the number of asylum requests). In the frontline states, indirect problem pressure may have also existed during the peak period: In Greece, most notably, even if they did not stay on, hundreds of thousands of refugees traveled across the country toward northern European destinations. Other member states temporarily closed their borders so as not to be directly concerned, or they used the occasion to tighten their asylum policy. During the long second wave of the crisis, we find peaks of policymaking in both types of member states, too. They are even more

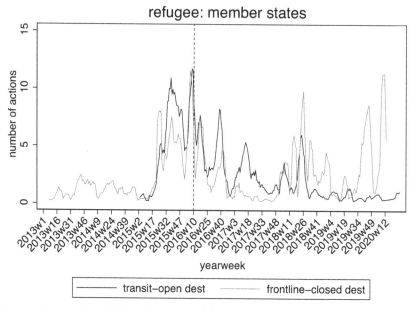

Figure 6 Time line of the salience of crisis-specific policymaking in the refugee crisis by type of member state: absolute weekly number of actions, thrice-weekly averages.

pronounced in the frontline and closed destination states. This pattern of policymaking salience suggests that it is not exclusively responding to problem pressure but is also likely to be induced by political entrepreneurs (H1f).

We pursue this question more systematically by analyzing the impact of our indicators for the problem and political pressure on crisis-specific policymaking during the different phases of the two crises at the national level. For this analysis, I use the episode-month and the country-week files, which provide monthly/weekly data on the number of actions. I combine second and third waves and distinguish between border control and asylum-integration policies for the refugee crisis and between border control-lockdown measures and all other policies for the COVID-19 crisis. I interact the two types of pressure with wave and policy to identify wave- and policy-specific effects. In addition, I introduce wave- and country-fixed effects and country-wave interactions, which allow controlling for all wave and country characteristics that are not directly related to the two types of pressure as measured by our indicators. The effects indicate the pressure-related variation within waves and countries regarding the salience of crisis-specific policymaking. For this analysis, the salience measure has been rescaled to the 0–1 range, which allows us to compare the effects across crises. Given that the pressure indicators are also rescaled to the 0–1 range, the effect parameters show the maximum impact of the two types of pressure on the salience of policymaking.

Figure 7 presents the results of this analysis.[11] Its first part refers to the variation of the effects across waves, while its second part presents the corresponding variation across policies. As is shown by the left-hand graph of Figure 7a, the direct impact of problem pressure on the salience of policymaking goes in the expected (positive) direction. Still, it is comparatively weak or nonsignificant in all waves during both crises. By contrast, the right-hand graph of this figure shows that the effect of political pressure (as measured by public salience) is substantial. This result confirms H1c. In the COVID-19 crisis, the impact of political pressure is most marked in the first wave and then decreases in the second and third waves. Although the effect dropped during the COVID-19 crisis, it was still quite sizeable in later waves: The renewed pressure during the later waves created new preoccupations in the public, which had a continued effect on the salience of policymaking. In the refugee crisis, the effect does not change much in the second wave, which is indicative of the impact of political entrepreneurs: In the absence of any effect of problem pressure, the continued impact of political pressure, as indicated by public salience, is very likely an endogenous effect of the politicization of the crisis in some countries – most notably in Hungary and Italy, but also in Germany.

Given that problem pressure and political pressure are linked, it is possible that problem pressure had an indirect impact on the salience of policymaking via political pressure (see Figure 2). An analysis of such a possible mediation effect (not shown) indicates that problem pressure does have a weak but significant indirect effect on the salience of policymaking during the peak phase of the refugee crisis and a highly significant impact during the second phase of this crisis, making for a still relatively weak, but significant total impact in the peak phase and a more substantial, but imprecise total effect in the second phase. In the case of the COVID-19 crisis, there are hardly any indirect effects at all, however. This means that even if we take indirect effects into account, the overall effect of problem pressure on the salience of policymaking is still comparatively weak, in any case, much weaker than the effect of political pressure. The weakness of the indirect effects of problem pressure contradicts our expectations and the structuralist reasoning.

Figure 7b shows that to the extent that problem pressure has any effect, it is limited to the salience of policymaking on *lockdown measures* in the COVID-19

---

[11] For details, see Table A1 in the online Appendix.

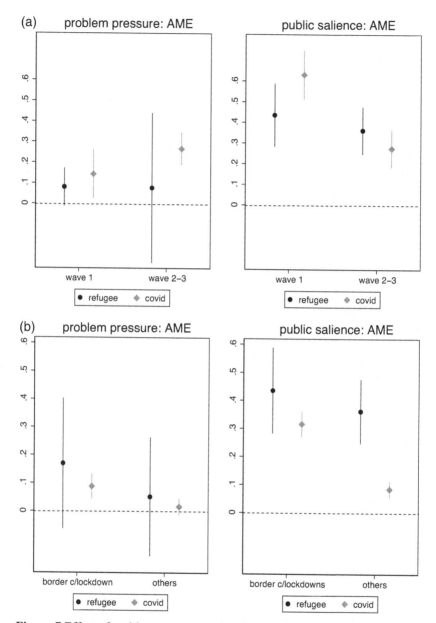

Figure 7 Effect of problem pressure and political pressure (public salience) on the salience of policymaking: Average marginal effects.

crisis. It does not affect other policy measures in this or the refugee crisis. As for the impact of political pressure, it is equally important for both types of policies in the refugee crisis but makes a big difference in the COVID-19 crisis: It has a powerful effect on *lockdown measures* but a much weaker effect on all other policy measures. These policy-specific effects during the COVID-19 crisis are in line with H1d: *The governments of every country immediately reacted to pressure from the public by taking border control and lockdown measures. In contrast, the remaining measures were less directly responsive.*

Finally, I also find country-specific differences concerning the salience of policymaking (H1g), which are not captured by our other indicators. Thus, during the refugee crisis, policymaking was most intense in Greece and least intense in the UK and Sweden during the peak phase: Greece, indeed, faced an exceptional kind of problem pressure, which is not captured by our indicator since most of the refugee arrivals moved on and did not stay in Greece. As a nonmember of Schengen, the UK was least concerned, and Swedish policy-makers reacted somewhat belatedly. We observe no country differences during the second wave of the refugee crisis. In the COVID-19 crisis, policymaking was most salient in Italy and Poland during the first phase. The pressure was extreme in Italy, where the pandemic hit first and particularly hard. As for Poland, eastern European countries generally reacted strongly in the first wave, i.e., were locking down early relative to the number of deaths caused by the virus. At the same time, they changed course later on, relaxing lockdowns and shifting to less restrictive measures with devastating effects on the mortality rates. Popic and Moise (2022) explain this particular response pattern in Eastern Europe as a combination of weak healthcare systems (inducing the governments to choose early lockdowns) and vulnerable economies (causing them to relax lockdowns more later on). In the second and third waves, policymaking in Poland was, indeed, least salient. At the same time, it was most salient in Germany, where the government struggled with the member state governments to impose its policy (Alexander 2021).

The Role of the Different Actors

The second set of results refers to the role of different actors in crisis management, which can be studied at both levels of the EU polity. At the national level, we can only rely on the four countries for which we have complete data on both crises. The results confirm the vital role of *executive decision-making* in crisis policymaking. Executive *actors* account for almost half (48 percent) of all policymaking action, and government executives account for no less than one-fourth (25 percent). In the absence of a benchmark outside of the two crises with which to compare these values, a German episode from the refugee crisis may serve as a proxy: In 2016, German policymakers adopted a new integration law, which was an essential piece of legislation that introduced an innovative new law, but which was only tangentially related to the refugee crisis and which in many ways represented a typical German legislative process. This episode mainly led to partisan conflicts between the members of the grand coalition and between them and the opposition. Executive decision-making accounted for 15 percent of the overall action in the episode, and government executives alone were responsible for 12 percent of all the actions. Taking these values as benchmarks, it is possible to appreciate executive decision-making's much more critical role in the two crises, confirming H2. The overall shares of this type of decision-making were very similar in both crises – 49 percent in the COVID-19 crisis and 45 percent in the refugee crisis. The corresponding shares for government executives were identical.

Figure 8 presents the percentage shares of executive actors – overall and governmental executives – in the two crises per wave and polity level. Comparing levels and crises jointly, we observe, as expected, that executive decision-making is more important at the EU level during the refugee crisis and more critical at the national level during the COVID-19 crisis. The differences are quite significant for the refugee crisis – 60 percent executive decision-making at the EU level compared to 42 percent at the national level – but more limited for the COVID-19 crisis – 43 percent at the EU and 50 percent at the national level. These results confirm that conflict management at the EU

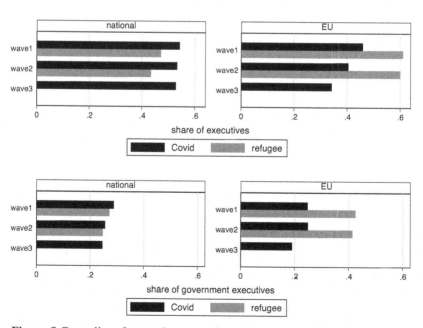

Figure 8 Centrality of executive actors by crisis, wave, and level: percentage shares.

level primarily involves executive decision-making. In contrast, at the national level, parties play a more significant role in conflict management (H2a). Contrary to expectations (H2b), the share of executive actors generally remains quite stable across waves and crises, except for the EU level during the COVID-19 crisis. Even in later waves of a crisis, executive policymaking remains the prevailing decision-making mode.

More generally, given the predominance of the intergovernmental coordination mode of decision-making, EU actors and national governments almost completely dominate crisis policymaking at the EU level. Their domination becomes apparent in Figure 9, which presents the centrality of actor types by crisis and level. These two actor types dominate in both crises. Still, their relative importance varies by crisis: EU actors were relatively more important during the COVID-19 crisis because this crisis concerned policy domains where the EU has greater competences (H2d). By contrast, governments were more significant in the refugee crisis, where they heavily clashed with each other, and transnational conflicts were more prominent (H2e). Among the remaining actors, only third countries and supranational actors, as well as civil society organizations, are of some significance at the EU level. Third countries and other supranational actors were of greater importance during the refugee crisis, which reflects the fact that the EU externalized problem solutions to third

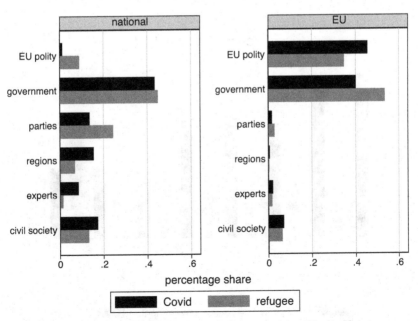

Figure 9 Centrality of actor types by crisis and level: percentage share.

countries during this crisis, most notably to Turkey, but also to Libya, or Morocco, as well as the fact that the EU was heavily clashing with UNHCR. The European Parliament and the parties represented there played virtually no role in crisis management at the EU level.

At the national level, governments are also the dominant actors, which align with the importance of executive decision-making. There are no differences in this respect between the two crises. National governments dominate crisis policymaking domestically, independently of the crisis. However, other actors are also important at the national level, albeit to different degrees, depending on the crisis. Thus, as expected by H2f, parties and EU-polity actors play a more significant role during the refugee crisis, reflecting the crisis's more conflictual character. By contrast, in the COVID-19 crisis, regional and local actors, experts, and civil society organizations stand out.

It is possible to investigate the impact of the *competence distribution* on the role actors play at the EU level more closely by distinguishing between three aggregate actor types: EU authorities, member state governments, and all other actors. Figure 10 presents the centrality of these three types of actors for the most important policies at the EU level. The policies are ordered from left to right according to the policy-specific centrality of EU authorities. As it turns out, the centrality of the EU authorities does not quite align with the policy-specific competence distribution between the two levels, although the latter has

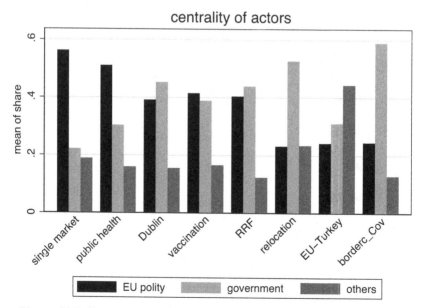

Figure 10 Policy-specific centrality of actors at the EU level: percentages.

an impact. Thus, EU authorities are most central in the single market domain, where they have most competence, while their role is most restricted in the case of border controls during the COVID-19 crisis, where the member states reigned supreme, benefiting from the exception rules in the Schengen scheme. The EU authorities also played a more limited role in the two most significant EU policies during the refugee crisis – the relocation scheme (plan A) and the EU–Turkey agreement (plan B), where member states enjoyed much greater autonomy. However, EU authorities have been central in public health, vaccination, and fiscal policy (RRF) – i.e., in domains with more limited competence. The reason for the differences between formal competence distributions and the observed centrality of EU authorities in the latter domains may be linked to "centralized coordination." This mode of coordination, which enhances the role of supranational actors while preserving the monitoring capacity of the member states, played a vital role in the joint vaccine procurement (Becker and Gehring 2023), in capacity building in the public health domain (Ferrera, Kyriazi, and Miró 2022), and in the negotiations for the RRF (Schelkle 2021).

The *transnational coalitions* are also expected to vary by crisis. Figure 11 presents the respective results. As we already know, EU actors dominate more in the COVID-19 than in the refugee crisis. The main reason for their lesser presence in the refugee crisis is the important role played by third countries and other

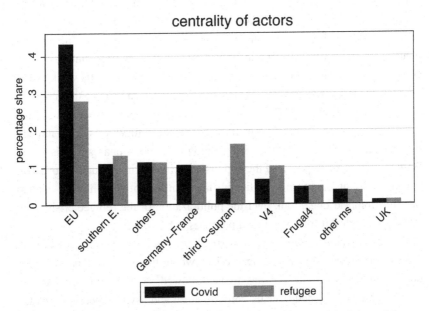

Figure 11 Centrality of transnational coalitions at the EU level, by crisis: percentage shares.

supranational actors, who are hardly present in the COVID-19 crisis. However, the prominence of the member states hardly varies between the crises at first sight. The multiple coalitions are almost equally present in both crises. The main differences concern the German–French coalition and the V4 coalition. The difference concerning the former does not become visible in the graph since it consists of the changing relative importance of the two countries in the two crises: As expected, Germany and the V4 coalition played a more significant role during the refugee crisis, whereas France was significantly more important during the COVID-19 crisis. The critical role of France corresponds to the increasing importance of the German–French coalition during the COVID-19 crisis, and the critical role of Germany and the V4 coalition reflects the driving role of Germany in the search for a joint solution to the refugee crisis, which met with the staunch opposition from the V4 coalition. Next to the German–French coalition, the southern Europeans constituted the most crucial coalition in both crises. They consistently asked for more solidarity among the member states, first in the context of the reform of the Dublin regulation, and then in the context of the economic catastrophe created by the COVID-19 crisis, especially in southern Europe. Similarly, the Frugal 4 were also present in both crises but to a lesser degree than the southern European countries. Although the graph does not capture this, their role was undoubtedly more significant during the COVID-19 crisis. The UK consistently played a minor role, as did all the other member states.

Finally, we briefly look at the role played by the various actor types at the national level (H2f). Figure 12 shows the corresponding variations for the four countries for which we have detailed information on both crises. The government is the most critical actor in both crises in all countries, but its role is comparatively weak in Germany during the COVID-19 crisis. Its weakness is a result of German federalism, which was crucial in managing this crisis in Germany (see Alexander 2021; Truchlewski et al. 2023). Conversely, the government played a vital role in Italy during the refugee crisis. As already mentioned, this derives from its composition in the later phases of this crisis: With the accession to power of the populist government in the summer of 2018, the government or, more specifically, the Minister of the Interior, Matteo Salvini, from the Lega, took over the politicization of the refugee crisis in an attempt to exploit it for his political purposes.

Finally, *party interventions* were particularly numerous in Germany in both crises, but especially in the refugee crisis, where the governing parties were deeply divided over the policies to be followed. As a result, the German government was divided over its border control and asylum measures. At the same time, it supported the (external) border control and asylum measures at the EU level, which ought to allow it to overcome its internal divisions.

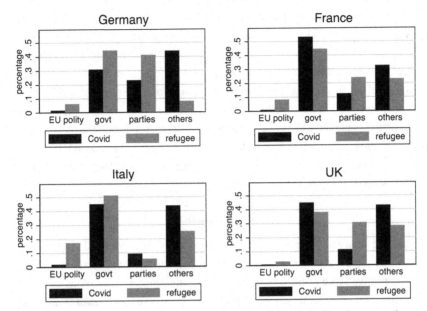

Figure 12 Centrality of actor types at the national level during the two crises: Germany, France, Italy, and the UK compared – percentages.

Conclusion

Regarding the salience of crisis policymaking and the centrality of specific actors in the policymaking process, there are many similarities between the two crises, even if policymaking during the COVID-19 crisis was much more salient than during the refugee crisis. In both crises and at both levels of the EU polity, the policymakers immediately responded to the exogenous shock. In both crises, they continued to respond to political pressure (i.e., public salience) throughout the crises, while the effect of problem pressure on policymaking was much more limited. Executive decision-making has characterized both crises, too. Due to the prevailing decision mode, EU authorities and member state governments dominated policymaking at the EU level. At the national level, it was the government that dominated. Finally, in both crises, EU-level policymaking was much more salient than policymaking in the average member state at the outset of the crises.

Differences between the two crises may appear secondary compared to these similarities. In later phases of the crises, policymaking tended to decline – more so during the refugee crisis than in the COVID-19 crisis, where later pandemic waves kept the policymakers busy. At the EU level, the relative importance of EU authorities and governments varied by crisis and policy domain, depending on the policy-specific competence distribution – a greater role for EU actors in economic policymaking during the COVID-19 crisis, a greater role of the governments (especially the German and V4 governments) and third countries during the refugee crisis. At the national level, the types of actors who played a central role in addition to the governments varied considerably: EU-polity actors and parties in the refugee crisis versus local–regional governments, experts, and civil society actors in the COVID-19 crisis. Moreover, political entrepreneurs played a significant role in some countries during the later phases of the refugee crisis, while their role was more limited in the COVID-19 crisis. As it turns out, these differences were highly consequential for policy support, which we will study in the next section.

5 Policy Support

I start the analysis with the overall support of policy proposals in the two crises by level and wave, for which I expect the two crises to differ considerably. Given the symmetric crisis situation, the extreme external pressure, the segmentation of policymaking at the two levels, and the limited politicization by parties, I expect greater general support in COVID-19 than in the refugee crisis (H3a). In addition, in the COVID-19, but not in the refugee crisis, I expect greater support early on due to the rally-around-the-flag effect (H3b). I do not expect such an effect in the refugee crisis, given that the policy domain was already highly politicized before the crisis set in. Figure 13 presents the corresponding effects for an OLS regression, including the direct and interaction effects between the three variables – crisis, level, and wave. The left-hand graph refers to the national level, and the right-hand graph to the EU level. For each level of the EU polity and each crisis, the graph also shows the average level of support, indicated by the corresponding dashed lines. Overall, at both levels of the polity, the level of support is higher in the COVID-19 than in the refugee crisis, which confirms our expectations. However, the difference in support is much more significant at the national level than at the EU level, where policy support was surprisingly high early in the refugee crisis.

At the national level, we find the expected rallying effect in the COVID-19 crisis, but, as expected, there is, indeed, no such rallying effect in the refugee crisis (H3a). In the COVID-19 crisis, the governments of the member states were the first to react, and they were the primary beneficiaries of the rallying effect. In the refugee crisis, by contrast, asylum policymaking at the national level had already been highly contentious before the exogenous shock, and the explosion of the crisis only exacerbated these already existing conflicts. The

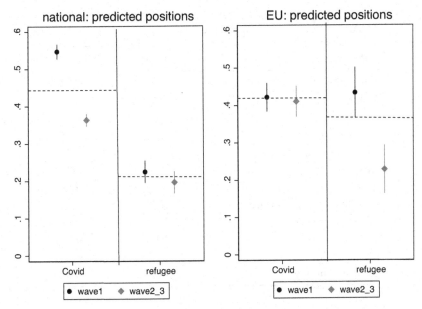

Figure 13 Support of crisis-specific policies, by crisis, level, and wave: predicted positions.

domestic blockades, especially in Germany, induced the decision-makers to search for alternative solutions at the EU level, where they first hit a blockade for their plan A (the relocation policy attempt). The surprisingly high support at the EU level is the result of the fact that the policymakers then could agree on a plan B, i.e., second-best solutions – reinforcement of the external border (ECBG) (Niemann and Speyer 2018), externalization (EU–Turkey agreement, EU–Libya agreement), and installation of hotspots in frontline states (Kriesi et al. 2024). Under the pressure of the crisis situation, there was an unexpected rallying effect at the EU level at the peak of the refugee crisis in support of stop-gap solutions despite the great contentiousness of the policy proposals. This effect was, however, not to the last. During the long second wave of the refugee crisis, the EU member states were unable to agree on a joint solution to reform the asylum policy, i.e., to a reform of the Dublin regulation, which is reflected in the equally low support of policy proposals at both polity levels during the second wave of the refugee crisis.

The greater contentiousness of the policymaking process in the refugee crisis is confirmed by a separate analysis of the explanatory power of the actors' positions in determining policy-specific support. The greater the share of variation in policy-specific backing, which can be attributed to the actors'

Table 3 Explanatory power of actor types for policy-specific support: R²adj.

Policy Domain	R2adj.	*n*
Relocation	0.62	281
Dublin reform	0.34	210
EU–Turkey	0.29	435
asylum-integration	0.27	3738
border closure, refugee	0.22	1211
RRF	0.23	815
fiscal	0.18	604
lockdown-border closure, covid	0.12	6701
single market	0.09	769
vaccination	0.08	3034
public health	0.08	3962
economic policy	0.07	3892

positions, the greater the conflicts between the actors, presumably. If there is no variation in the actors' positions, i.e., if the actors are more or less consensual concerning domain-specific policy proposals, then the actors' positions cannot account for policy support at all. To assess the contentiousness of the various policy domains, we predict the policy-specific support by the actors' positions, the waves, and the interactions between the two, as the actors' positions may vary from one wave to the other.

As is documented in Table 3, the explanatory power of the actors' positions (i.e., conflicts between them) is generally higher for the refugee crisis policy domains than for the COVID-19 crisis corresponding domains. The one exception concerns fiscal policy. Both at the EU (the RRF) and the national level (fiscal policy), the conflicts in fiscal policy reach an intensity that is comparable with the lowest policy-specific conflict intensity of the refugee crisis (for border closures). However, in the remaining policy domains of the COVID crisis, the share of the variance in policy support explained by differences in actors' positions is rather limited. In the refugee crisis, the relocation scheme is an extreme case, as the actors' positions account for no less than roughly two-thirds of the variation in question. This analysis confirms the devastating effect of this proposal on the relations between the policymakers. The Dublin reform turns out to be the second most contentious policy domain in this crisis, which doubtlessly contributed to the fact that such a (restricted) reform has only become possible very late in the day (spring 2024).

The Role of Executive Actors and Exogenous Pressure

Following Schattschneider (1975), I expect policy support to increase as a function of the extent to which executive actors control the policymaking process (H3). This expectation is based on two claims. First, it assumes that policy support by executive actors is decisive for overall support. In line with this assumption, the correlation between general and executive actors' support is very close. At the EU level, it varies between .84 for the six episodes of the refugee crisis and .98 for the six-issue domains in the COVID-19 crisis. The correlations for the episodes at the member state level are .89 and .92, respectively, for the two crises. Second, it assumes that executive actors generally lend more support to the policies than other types of actors. The first row of graphs in Figure 14 shows that this assumption holds for the national level in both crises but not at the EU level. At the EU level, there seems to be little difference between the executive and other actors in this respect in both crises. As the two graphs in the second row show, however, the support by executive actors varies by policy at the EU level, depending on the contentiousness of the policy. Thus, in the case of the two most contentious episodes during the refugee crisis, the reform of the Dublin regulation and, even more extreme, the relocation scheme, executive actors were more opposed to the proposal than the other actors. This results from conflicts at the EU level, mainly between governments of member states, represented by the top executives of transnational coalitions in joint decision-making. By contrast, executive actors favored the consensual EU–Turkey agreement more than other actors. In the consensual COVID crisis, support by executive actors was higher than support by different actors in two domains – vaccination and border control; in the other policy domains, there was hardly any difference in the support between the two.

At the national level, it is possible to systematically analyze the effect of problem pressure, political pressure, salience, and the role of actors on policy support using the episode-month and the long country-week files. For the COVID-19 crisis, but not for the refugee crisis, we expect problem and political pressure to enhance policy support by policymakers throughout the crisis (H3c). In contrast, more significant pressure in the refugee crisis will likely lead to more intense politicization and enhance the underlying conflict. The systematic analysis bears out these expectations. However, as shown in Figure 15[12] for the COVID-19 crisis, greater support *only occurs when problem pressure and public salience combine* to exert

---

[12] Detailed results can be found in Table A2 in the online Appendix. The results for the refugee crisis are based on contemporaneous effects, while the results for the COVID-19 crisis are based on a dynamic analysis using the stata procedure xtpmg. The dynamic results show the long-run effects of the various predictors.

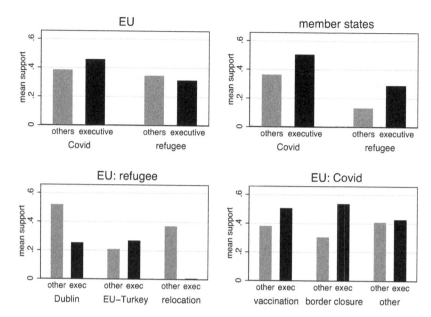

Figure 14 Support of crisis-specific policies by crisis, level, and executive actors: average level of support.

a powerful thrust on policymakers. In the absence of public salience, problem pressure hurts policy support. However, if both types of pressure are intense, policymakers rally strongly around government proposals in the COVID-19 crisis. As expected, for the refugee crisis, we do not find any effects of pressure on support, whether positive or negative.

In addition, this analysis confirms that *executive actors* enhance the overall policy support in both crises (H3). I did not formulate any hypotheses regarding the effect of salience of policymaking, but the results indicate that it is not associated with policy support. The two vary independently: Intensely debated policy proposals may be equally supported/resisted as proposals that pass virtually unnoticed. Finally, these results also show that in the refugee crisis support is more significant in later waves, contrary to the rallying effect, but in line with the notion that this crisis hit a policy domain that was already highly politicized initially. Moreover, asylum-integration policy was less supported than border control measures during this crisis.

Policy Support at the EU Level

I have argued that member states are the critical actors at the EU level and that their resistance is policy-specific and organized into transnational coalitions (H3e). We can approach this issue in two steps: First, I show the policy-specific

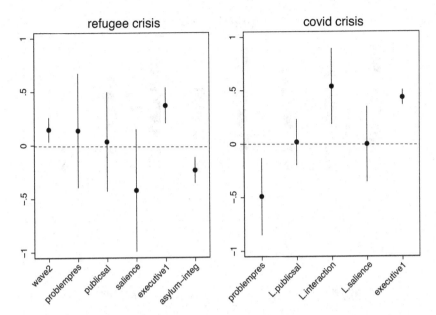

Figure 15 Effects of problem pressure, public salience, and crisis characteristics on the support of policymaking, the refugee crisis, and COVID crisis, predicted contemporary (refugee crisis) and long-run (COVID-19 crisis) support.

support by three types of actors – EU authorities, member state governments, and other actors, the role of which I already analyzed in Figure 10. Then, I document, in more detail, the support of the different policies by the transnational coalitions. Figure 16 presents the average policy-specific support by the three actor types and clarifies who was the most critical for EU proposals. The policies are the same as in Figure 10, but they are now ordered from left (low support) to right (high support) according to the support they received from member state governments. Unsurprisingly, EU authorities supported all the proposals except border control during the COVID-19 crisis, where they did not have much to say. In this exceptional case, they could only warn the member states that border closures would run the risk of fragmentation of the single market and undermine free movement and supply chains.

Support by member states, however, varies substantially from the relocation scheme and the Dublin reform, which were opposed by a majority of the member states or received not much support from them, to the border control policies in the COVID-19 crisis, and the EU–Turkey agreement, which they widely supported. The contrast between the relocation scheme (plan A) and the EU–Turkey agreement (plan B) during the refugee crisis is striking. Having rejected the EU's plan A, the member states came around in support of the EU's plan B, but they stuck to

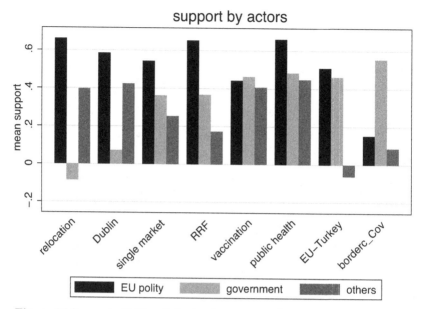

Figure 16 Support of EU policies by three types of actors: average support.

their opposition concerning the relocation scheme and the long-term Dublin reform. They supported a stop-gap solution (the EU–Turkey agreement, as well as the ECBG and the hotspot approach (not shown in Figure 16)), which alleviated the problem pressure but reduced the incentives for long-term reform. In contrast, they endorsed proposals in all policy domains in the COVID crisis, contributing to successful problem-solving.

Figure 17 presents more details regarding the positions of transnational coalitions in selected policy domains. I have chosen the six most important policy domains: single market policies, the RRF, vaccination policy for the COVID-19 crisis, the relocation scheme, the EU–Turkey agreement, and Dublin reform for the refugee crisis. The figure presents the average policy-specific support by the various transnational coalitions, provided they undertook more than three actions in a given wave and policy at the EU level. For the Dublin reform and vaccination policy, I do not distinguish by waves because most of the action in these domains centered on the second/third waves. I keep Germany and France apart because they do not always share the same positions.

In the generally consensual COVID-19 crisis, the single market policies were most consensual across transnational coalitions, except for Germany, which appears least supportive of the economic measures at the EU level. The German exception is primarily due to the German Constitutional Court ruling, which squeezed the ECB because of its bond-buying programs.[13] In the case of the RRF, the situation is more mixed (see Table 3). There was, after all, opposition to adopting the RRF, which rendered the negotiations at the July 2020 summit most difficult (Schelkle 2021; Truchlewski et al. 2023: Chapter 8). The Frugal 4 opposed the proposal in the first wave, and during the ratification phase (second wave), the V4 coalition opposed it even more vigorously. However, the RRF received strong support from the EU authorities, the German–French leadership, and the southern European member states. In the negotiation process, the Frugal 4 coalition gave up its opposition to the grant component of the fund and no longer objected to the proposal in the ratification phase of the RRF, as shown in Figure 17.

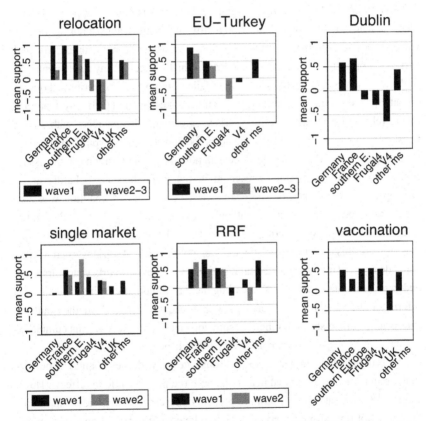

Figure 17 Policy-specific support by actors and wave, at the EU level: average support.

[13] Martin Arnold and Tommy Stubbington: German Court calls on ECB to justify bond-buying program, FT, May 5, 2020.

Hungary was the main protagonist in the conflict around the ratification of the RRF, which was dominated by the rule-of-law debate (Bohle, Greskovits, and Naczyk 2023). Poland was its closest ally, and the rest of the member states opposed both countries. Together, the two countries objected to linking the attribution of grants and loans in the framework of the RRF to the rule-of-law mechanism. This link was proposed by the Commission and supported by most member states and the European Parliament (EP). Resistance also came from other actors, particularly opposition parties in the first wave. But this opposition was negligible. Third, the vaccination graph shows broad support for the joint procurement policy. The UK government was the only actor opposed to this policy, but its opposition did not matter since it was already on the way out of the Union.

The relocation scheme starkly contrasts with these three policy domains from the COVID-19 crisis. As the respective graphs show, it was widely supported by the member states (in addition to help from the EU authorities), at least during the first wave of the refugee crisis, i.e., the peak phase. However, it met with extreme and very vocal opposition from the V4 countries, which boycotted any implementation of the joint scheme. Once the scheme had failed, support for it deteriorated during the later phases of the crisis among all member states, even in Germany. Contrary to the relocation scheme, the EU–Turkey agreement did not meet with strong resistance. Germany was the driving force behind it, and the southern frontline states supported it. Many member states did not take strong positions on this issue: France, for example, is not represented in the graph because it hardly at all participated in the debate on the deal with Turkey. The V4 coalition was also somewhat opposed to this agreement, but its opposition was not as vocal as in the relocation scheme. Many critiques came from the Frugal 4 (essentially from Austria), but this critique came late and was not decisive. Austria warned against dependency on Turkey, criticized human rights violations in Turkey, and urged an end to accession talks with Turkey, calling them a "diplomatic fiction." Finally, the reform of the Dublin regulation met with broad resistance from the southern European frontline states, northern destination states, and the V4. This cumulated resistance gave any reform proposal very little chance.

The refugee crisis, in particular, demonstrates how domestic and EU policy-making may be closely linked in a crisis, with reciprocal spillover effects (H3e). Figure 18 illustrates this point. It presents the estimated policy support of various actor types for each crisis at the two levels.[14] First, the figure documents the German predicament during the refugee crisis. Because of its internal divisions, the German government ("Germany") was not supportive of its

---

[14] These estimates are based on straight-forward OLS regressions, which predict support based on actor type, polity level, and the interaction between the two variables. See Table A3 in the online Appendix.

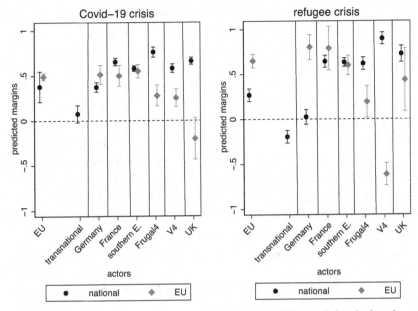

Figure 18 Policy support by actors for national and EU policies during the COVID-19 and the refugee crisis: predicted support.

national policy proposals but highly supportive of the EU-level proposals. It strongly promoted the EU proposals as a substitute for its contentious national policies. As the German government was internally divided and struggled to deal with the crisis domestically, it pressured the other member states to get the relocation quota passed in the Council of the EU to alleviate its burden. However, the adoption of the relocation scheme, pushed through by the Germans in September 2015, turned into a fiasco, from which European asylum policy never recovered (van Middelaar 2017: 110). From this point on, in Eastern Europe, accepting refugees was viewed not as a humanitarian act but as a submission to Berlin. It was only once Germany had failed to obtain a working relocation scheme from its fellow member states that it turned to an agreement with Turkey as the second-best solution. In the summer of 2018, when the border control issue returned to German politics, German policy-making once again spilled over to the EU level (see Figure 5).

Figure 18 shows the opposite combination for the V4 countries, where the governments strongly endorsed their domestic policies during the refugee crisis but forcefully opposed the corresponding policies at the EU level. While the German predicament undermined the government's leadership role at the EU level, the solid domestic stance of the V4 governments strengthened their critical hand at the EU level. The figure also shows that the Frugal 4 (i.e., primarily

Austria) were generally critical of the EU's policies during the refugee crisis. At the same time, their governments enjoyed strong support at the national level. In addition, the figure indicates comparatively low support of national policies by EU actors and the opposition of transnational actors to national policies during the refugee crisis. Both types of actors from the EU polity had to deal with the negative externalities of unilateral policies, as already pointed out before. Compared to the refugee crisis, such spillover effects were much more contained during the COVID-19 crisis because of the reciprocal character of the external-ities of member state actions. In the COVID-19 crisis, policymaking at the two levels of the EU polity was segmented, which is an additional reason for the absence of conflict among policymakers in this crisis. The only two exceptions concern the spillover of the rule-of-law crisis into the ratification of the RRF (which could be contained) and the unilateral British vaccination policy (which had little effect since the UK was already on its way out).

Policy Support at the Member State Level

Moving to the domestic level, I analyze the support by the various actor types in the two crises based on the four countries, for which we have complete data on both crises. The overall results, controlling for country, wave, and policy domain, are presented in Figure 19 for six actor types: EU-polity actors, governments, regional and local authorities, governing and opposition parties, and civil society actors.[15] For governments and ruling parties, I additionally distinguish between Germany and the three other countries because of the specific intragovernmental conflicts in Germany during the refugee crisis. I do not show results for the COVID-19 crisis for EU-polity actors because there are too few cases – a result of the just mentioned segmentation of the two levels in this crisis. The results essentially, although not wholly, confirm H3f, which expects greater support among all nonexecutive actors during the COVID-19 crisis: regional and local actors, civil society actors in general, and the German government/German governing parties in particular are, indeed, more support-ive of the government in the COVID-19 than in the refugee crisis. For govern-ments and governing parties other than the German ones and opposition parties, there are only minor differences between the two crises: Governments generally support their proposals independently of the crisis in question, and opposition parties oppose them, undaunted by whether the crisis poses an existential threat to the country or not. However, in line with expectations, opposition parties are less vocal during the less conflictual COVID-19 crisis – they account for only 7.3 percent of all actions, compared to 12.4 percent during the refugee crisis. As

---

[15] For details, see Table A4 in the online Appendix.

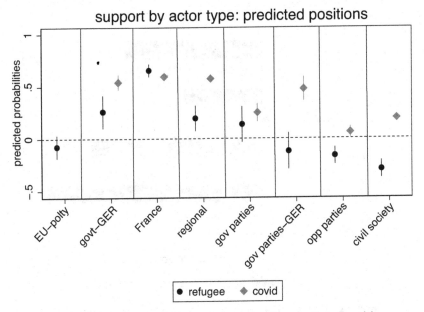

Figure 19 Policy support by actor type and crisis: predicted positions.

we have already seen, EU-polity actors are somewhat critical of national policies in the case of the refugee crisis.

Finally, I turn to *country differences* (H3g). As shown in Figure 20, the government's policy proposals found more support in the COVID-19 crisis than in the refugee crisis in three out of the four countries. The differences are particularly stark in Germany, where the government proposals found broad resistance in the refugee crisis but (weak) support during the COVID-19 crisis, and in Italy, where the support of the government's proposals was also fragile during the refugee crisis. The exception is France, where the government's proposals were equally supported in both crises. In the two crises, the French government received roughly average support (indicated by the dashed line). This is not surprising as far as the COVID-19 crisis is concerned. For the refugee crisis, the relatively strong support of the French government is likely to be explained by the fact that France was a closed destination state, which was not directly concerned by the inflow of refugees in 2015–16. The same applies to the UK, which was also a closed destination state and which, as a nonmember of the Schengen area, was even less concerned by the refugee crisis than France. In the case of the UK, what is somewhat surprising is the government's strong support during the COVID-19 crisis. This strong support is surprising because the UK initially faced a worse pandemic than other European countries, partly because of the government's fault. The British government did change course

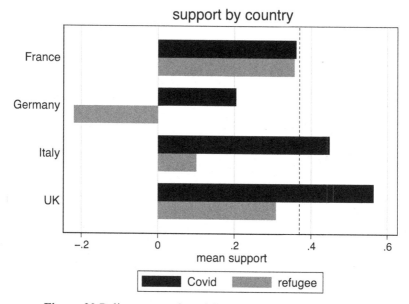

Figure 20 Policy support by crisis and country, mean support.

after initially accepting the virus's spread, which would build herd immunity. We can only speculate that the high level of support for the British government's policies was linked to the Brexit negotiation process, which overlapped with the COVID-19 crisis: The UK officially left the EU on January 31, 2020, which opened a transition period that was going to last until the end of 2020, i.e., deep into the second COVID-19 wave, during which the two parties – the EU and the UK – negotiated the Trade and Cooperation Agreement that was to regulate their future relationship (Laffan and Telle 2023: Chapter 8). It is likely that, in the UK, this ongoing negotiation process reinforced the rallying effect of the COVID-19 crisis beyond the first wave.

Figure 21 presents the support of the government's proposals *per wave* in the two crises. We observe a rallying effect early on during the COVID-19 crisis in all four countries. For reasons I have just speculated about, this rallying effect was kept up in the UK during the later waves of the crisis. The continued rallying effect in the UK may have also resulted from the fact that the UK was initially more effective in vaccine procurement than the EU (Becker and Gehring 2023). By contrast, there was no rallying effect during the refugee crisis in any country. The seeming rallying effect in Italy is primarily a consequence of a change in governments during the crisis and of the fact that it was most concerned with reforming the Dublin regulation, which only became an important issue during the second part of the crisis.

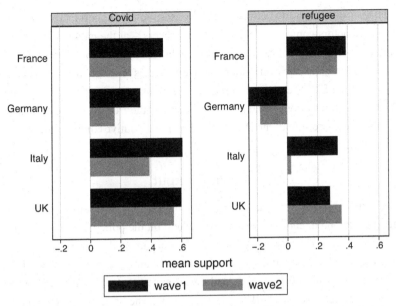

Figure 21 Policy support by crisis, country, and wave: mean support.

Conclusion

Regarding policy support, the differences between the two crises prevail. The existential threat in general, the relative symmetry of the crisis incidence transnationally, and the comparative absence of partisan politicization domestically made the COVID-19 crisis much more consensual than the refugee crisis. The consensus manifests itself at both levels of EU policymaking, especially early on when there is a rallying effect in the COVID-19 crisis, but not in the refugee crisis. To be sure, we also observe a rallying effect at the EU level during the refugee crisis, but it is deceptive because it extends only to the second-best solutions, whereas the preferred solution met with powerful resistance from some transnational coalitions. At the national level, combined problem pressure and public salience enhanced policy support in the COVID-19 crisis but not in the refugee crisis. Moreover, all nonexecutive actors supported the government's proposals more during the COVID-19 pandemic than during the refugee crisis, except for the partisan opposition, which was, however, less vocal during the pandemic than during the refugee crisis. Policy support at the two levels is closely linked by spillover effects in the refugee crisis but not in the COVID-19 crisis, where policymaking at the two levels was broadly segmented. The spillover effects during the refugee crisis reflect the conflictive character of policymaking in this crisis. In contrast, the segmentation of policymaking contributes to the consensual character of policymaking in the COVID-19 crisis.

There is one similarity between the two crises: Policy support increases as the executive actors control the policymaking process – at the national level. The situation is more complicated at the EU level since the national governments call the shots at the EU level, and their top executives represent them. Executive support at the EU level depends on the contentiousness of the policy proposal. Thus, in the highly conflictual policy proposals at the EU level – the relocation scheme and the reform of the Dublin regulation – executive control is associated with a lack of support.

6 Policy Output

In this last empirical section, I am focusing on the policy output, i.e., the policy measures adopted, and only to a limited extent on the policy outcome, i.e., the impact on the very problem pressure at the origin of the crises – inflow of refugees and their integration into the national community in the case of the refugee crisis, and infection and death rates as well as growth rates and public debt in the case of the COVID-19 crisis. Whether the policy response adopted by the policymakers serves to reduce the problem pressure and puts an end to the crisis depends not only on the policy response but also on the cooperation of the population (e.g., testing rates and use of contact tracing apps in the case of the pandemic) and on the capacity of the member states to implement the policies. In contrast, the policy output largely depends on policymaking. I first look at the policy output at the EU level and then analyze the output at the level of the member states.

Policy Output at the EU Level

At the EU level, the favorable policy output in the COVID-19 crisis, which contrasts with the minimal policy output in the refugee crisis, confirms the role of support in facilitating joint solutions (H4, H4a). Given the more favorable conditions of the crisis situation, EU authorities' support was more significant in the COVID-19 crisis. Joint action became possible in the public health and the economic policy domain (see Jones, Daniel Kelemen, and Meunier 2021; Quaglia and Verdun 2023; Rhodes 2021; Schelkle 2021; Truchlewski et al. 2023). As we have seen, transnational coalitions opposed the RRF's proposals, but the German–French leadership overcame this resistance (H4e). The most significant advances were made in the economic policy domain, where the EU already had the most critical competencies – the integrated market is one of its core competencies, and monetary policy is in the hands of the ECB. The response came early in the economic policy domain and diminished in later waves, as H4b expected. In this domain, the crisis induced an accommodating monetary policy and regulatory measures, such as suspending SGP and competition rules, to give the member states free reign in their fiscal, economic, and social policy responses to the crisis. In addition, it also led to centralized capacity building in the form of SURE, an instrument for temporary support to mitigate unemployment risks in an emergency, and above all, in the form of the RRF, an investment fund above all designed to improve the economic capacity of the weaker member states. The SURE instrument helped more fragile member states finance short-time work schemes to deal with the immediate fallout of the economic shock of the pandemic. The fiscal permissiveness of the EU during the COVID-19 crisis indirectly also increased the capacity of the weaker member states to come to terms with the economic shock. The RRF, an investment fund of unique proportions, is expected to create a level playing field between the member states in the long run. Even if it is too early to tell whether this example of centralized capacity building is of a permanent or only of a temporary nature (Fabbrini 2022), and even if its implementation may turn out to have been less effective than initially intended (Boeri and Perrotti 2023), the adoption of the RRF in July 2020 has been a watershed moment in EU fiscal governance.

In the public health domain, the timing of the policy response, which was most important in later waves, contradicts H4b to some extent. The minimal competencies of the EU may explain this unexpected result in this policy domain, which limited its policy responses early on. The continued pressure exerted by the crisis helped to extend its competencies in later waves (H4c). In the first COVID-19 wave, the EU had a limited impact on national decisions to close borders and control entry. The lack of EU coordination encouraged member states to go it alone or copy their peers under the pressure of the crisis. As the pressure was kept up in the later waves, the EU engaged in comprehensive coordination with new instruments (e.g., the Green Pass and traffic light systems for traveling). Initially, the EU also failed to prevent unilateral measures by member states in the public health domain (e.g., unilateral export bans for medical). Still, it eventually made up for its initial failures with its joint vaccine procurement program. Although lagging behind the United States and the UK in its common vaccine procurement strategy, the EU quickly caught up in the spring and summer of 2021. EU member states managed to coordinate in pooling funds for access to vaccines (apart from Hungary and Slovakia, which also unilaterally relied on Chinese and Russian vaccines). In addition, in the realm of health policy, the EU also proceeded to build institutional capacities by creating components of a "European Health Union" – HERA (European Health Emergency Response Authority) and an EHU (European Health Union), while also expanding the mandates of the ECDC (European Center for Disease

Control) and the EMA (European Medicines Agency) (Ferrera, Kyriazi, and Miró 2022).

COVID-19 also contributed to EU capacity building, i.e., polity maintenance, beyond the policy domains directly concerned by the crisis. Thus, it affected the "rule-of-law" crisis, which originated from two member states – Hungary and Poland – that introduced illiberal institutional reforms in violation of central European values. The EU proceeded to sanction these two deviant member states by not allowing them to benefit from the RRF funds attributed to them as long as they did not reform their legal institutions. Moreover, in procedural terms, as already mentioned, Ladi and Wolff (2021: 36) argue that a policymaking mode emerged from the EU's institutional response to the COVID-19 crisis, best described as "coordinative Europeanization." This coordination mode is neither purely intergovernmental nor exclusively supra-national since it involves direct consultations between member states and the Commission to elaborate policies that would work for everyone. Interestingly, similar coordination mechanisms have been applied in the joint vaccine pro-curement during the COVID-19 crisis (Becker and Gehring 2023), in the capacity building in the public health domain (Ferrera, Kyriazi, and Miró 2022), and in the Brexit negotiations (Laffan and Telle 2023). Ferrera, Kyriazi, and Miró (2022) use "expansive unification" to characterize these new coordination mechanisms.

The policy output at the EU level during the refugee crisis starkly contrasts with the production during the COVID-19 crisis. The combination of asymmet-rical incidence and joint competence between EU and member states with partisan politicization at the domestic level proved to be particularly critical for common solutions. As I have shown, such a setting renders joint policy-making initiatives and collective action difficult and, instead, leads to unilateral reactions on the part of member states, the spillover effects of which unleash and exacerbate transnational conflicts and give rise to a complex web of cross-level and transnational interactions to come to terms with these conflicts. As a result of these difficulties, the EU failed to adopt the relocation scheme, which was blocked by the V4 coalition, and, as was already pointed out in the previous section, it had to rely on the stop-gap solution of the EU–Turkey agreement, which was made possible by the joint efforts of the German Chancellor and her allies among the EU authorities. Moreover, despite the pressure exerted by the crisis, the EU proved unable to reform its defective asylum policy for many years after the peak of the crisis. Instead, it limited access to the Common European Asylum System (CEAS) (Lavenex 2018) by reinforcing its external borders and by externalizing the problem solution to third countries. The EU has been buying time by relying on "defensive integration" (Schimmelfennig

2021). Still, the incapacity to reform the standard asylum policy led to reactivating the conflict potentials linked to asylum and migration policy at subsequent times. In this policy domain, the EU seems stuck in a "sub-optimal equilibrium" (Hix and Hoyland 2022: 363).

Alexander Shaw, Kovarek, and Schelkle (2024) asked a series of experts on European integration – academics and policymakers – about the consequences of four crises – the COVID-19 crisis, the refugee crisis, the Euro Area crisis, and the Brexit crisis – for European integration. Their results align with the summary of the two crises I have compared here. They show that the refugee crisis is overwhelmingly perceived as having had negative consequences for integration (by 85 percent of respondents). In comparison, the COVID-19 pandemic is overwhelmingly seen as having a positive effect on integration (by 70 percent of the respondents). The other two crises are situated in between.

Policy Output at the Member State Level: Refugee Crisis

At the national level, too, continuity prevailed in the refugee crisis. The measures introduced during this crisis were consistent with an approach that can be traced back over two decades (Geddes, Hadj Abdou, and Brumat 2020). The intense partisan politicization of the policies involved limited policy support and prevented any significant steps forward (H4, H4a). At the national level, the crisis pressure during the refugee crisis primarily led to the reintroduction of domestic border controls and further retrenching of asylum policy across member states. The national policy response varied, above all, according to the member state type (H4e). Thus, frontline states turning a blind eye to secondary movements of refugees created border conflicts with neighboring states (e.g., Italy with Austria and France or France with the UK). Unilateral border closures created conflicts with humanitarian organizations and other member states, such as in the case of the Italian port closures for NGO ships saving refugees or in the cases of Hungarian and Austrian fence building at their southern borders. Border issues poisoned domestic politics in Germany, where they openly divided the government throughout the crisis. As for retrenching asylum policy, it generally attempted to make the member states less attractive for asylum seekers in different ways. Thus, Sweden, the paradigmatic open destination state, introduced temporal limits (three years) to residence permits for asylum seekers, aligning itself with other member states that already had such limits. Austria introduced an "upper limit" for the number of asylum seekers it would accept annually. Germany adopted two asylum packages to make life more difficult for asylum seekers. France and the UK, closed destination states, generally aimed at creating a "hostile environment" for asylum seekers (see Kriesi et al. 2024).

The impact of the national policy output on the intended outcome is difficult to gauge, i.e., the impact of these measures on their intended goal to stop the inflow of asylum seekers on the national territory. It is the EU–Turkey agreement that essentially stopped the inflow in the 2015–16 crisis: The member states were rescued by the EU in the short run, in an illustration of Alan Milward's general thesis (Milward 2000). The national measures were not particularly relevant to stopping the inflow but remained essentially symbolic politics. Thus, to mention but this example, the preset Austrian upper limit – a European precedent, the provision for a quantitative limit to grant a human right (Gruber 2017: 51) – has never been reached, meaning the corresponding decree was never applied.

Importantly, however, the refugee crisis had a more general political impact (see Kriesi et al. 2024). The political parties on the right have been reinforced by a general drift toward the right resulting from this crisis, even if the crisis did not give rise to a wholesale transformation of party systems in any country, as was the case in the Euro Area crisis. In contrast to the Euro Area crisis, which caught several actors by surprise or forced them to adopt untenable and unpopular positions, the refugee crisis, with its cumulative and expected nature, allowed much more room for strategic choices by parties that were able to anticipate the potential political impact of the crisis and react strategically to the country-specific crisis situation. The most salient transformation pattern is a drift toward the right, as more parties on this side of the spectrum rushed to capitalize on the issue and prioritize it in their campaign discourse. Right-wing actors who persisted in their anti-immigration message enjoyed electoral gains at the expense of their proximate competitors and of the left. In some countries, such as Hungary, Austria, the UK, and Greece, nationalist conservative parties displaced the radical right, while in others, such as Italy, Germany, France, and Sweden, the radical right increased its vote share at the expense of the mainstream right. The drift to the nationalist–conservative right, the exacerbation of the conflict between nationalists and cosmopolitans at the domestic level, and the transnational conflicts between a sovereignty coalition and a core coalition bent on further integration suggest that the refugee crisis has generally undermined the solidarity between member states in the EU.

Policy Output at the Member State Level: COVID-19 Crisis

At the beginning of the COVID-19 crisis, the member states reigned supreme. The fear and panic generated by the images from Italy sent shockwaves throughout the Union. Border control was in their competence, as was the public health policy. Given the great uncertainty at the outset of the pandemic, governments thought they could buy time by closing borders to slow the spread of the virus in the first wave. Except for a few controversial outliers, notably Sweden (and the Netherlands at the beginning of the pandemic), member states adopted widespread lockdowns through regulatory convergence. They required various forms of social distancing, independently of how hard the virus hit them. They quickly adopted high-cost policies such as work and school closures. In contrast, practices later deemed relatively low-cost and highly effective at reducing the spread of the virus, such as screening and contact tracing, were comparatively slower to implement (Mistur, Givens, and Matisoff 2023). This regulatory convergence occurred spontaneously rather than as a consequence of the EU and its coordination mechanisms (Truchlewski et al. 2023). Lockdowns shut down economic and public life at the national level. Again, the member states were the first to react to the economic catastrophe these measures implied. If solidarity was the word of the hour, it was solidarity within the nation-states. The nation-state made an economic comeback. Across Europe, member state governments opened the fiscal spigots: fiscal activism replaced austerity. The measures they adopted were temporary emergency measures, ranging from liquidity support for enterprises to short-term wage schemes and schemes for the income of the self-employed. When the emergency subsided, they were phased out, only to be renewed, extended, and adjusted as the pandemic struck once again in subsequent waves. At the end of the first wave, short-term recovery came sooner and has been far faster than expected initially. As lockdowns ended and economies recovered, it became essential to shift policies toward promoting recovery and to prevent the mistake of the 2008 financial crisis of switching too soon from support toward fiscal consolidation and monetary tightening. In the end, one needed to move from recovery to long-term expansion.

For the analysis of national policy output during the COVID-19 crisis, I can rely on three well-defined indicators. As mentioned in the design section, they include a general indicator for the government's response, an indicator for the stringency of the government's lockdown measures, and an indicator for the economic response, each ranging from 0 to a maximum of 100. These indicators allow us to systematically analyze the link between the crisis situation, policymaking, and policy output. You will find the time line of the responses for the three indicators in Figure 22, by country and as a country mean. As seen from these time lines, the response pattern did not vary much from one member state to the other. They immediately responded in public health and economic terms when the crisis hit. At the end of the first wave, they all relaxed their public health and stringency response while keeping up the economic support. After an intermediate period, the public health and stringency response was stepped up

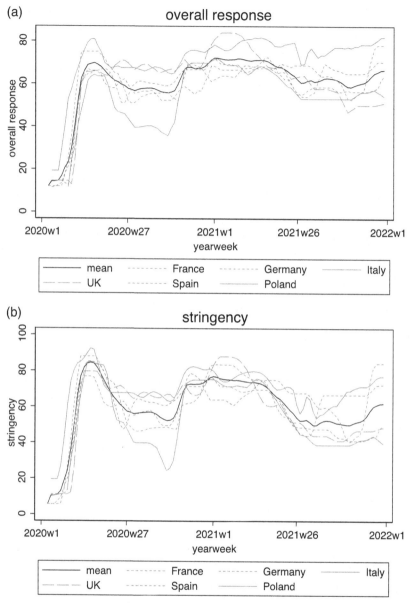

Figure 22 Time line of policy response of member states' policy response, by country and overall mean. The indicators have been smoothed by running averages over three weeks.

again in the second wave and only relaxed a second time in the second half of 2021. The continuing high level of policy response contradicts H4b, which expected declining policy output throughout the crisis. It is the continuing

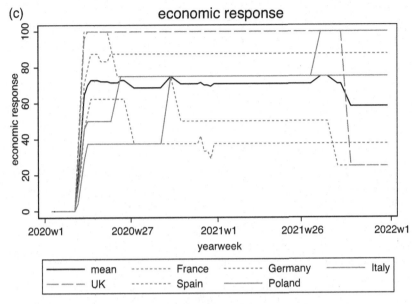

(c)

Figure 22 (cont.)

pressure that keeps up the pace of policymaking: Problem pressure increases again massively at the beginning of the second wave, and public salience remains high throughout the three waves (see Figure 3b).

Poland is the country that deviates most in the less restrictive direction. It stands here as an example for Eastern European countries. As already pointed out in Section 4, this particular response pattern in Eastern Europe can be explained by the vulnerable economies of these countries inducing them to relax lockdowns more in later phases of the pandemic (see Popic and Moise 2022). On the other side, Italy has the most robust overall response. It was hit early on, reacted faster and more strongly than the other member states, and kept up its general reaction until the end of 2021.

The similarity of the policy response patterns across member states during the COVID-19 crisis already points to the significant impact of the problem and political pressure on the polity output: The crisis situation did not leave the policymakers much room for choice of their reactions, it seems. This hunch can be tested with a more systematic analysis of the determinants of the policy output during this crisis. To predict the overall government response, I use the pressure indicators and the general characteristics of policymaking – its salience, executive dominance, and policy support as predictors. For the stringency of the lockdown and the economic policy response, I rely on the corresponding

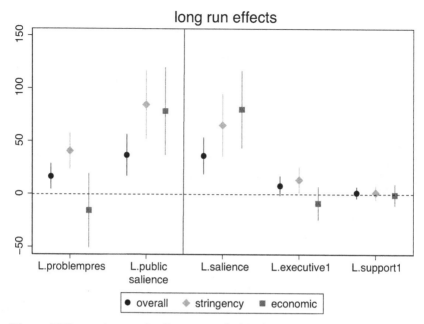

Figure 23 Determinants of policy output during the COVID-19 crisis: long-run effects.

attributes of the lockdowns (restrictions and relaxations)/public health domains, as well as the economic policy domain. Figure 23 presents the effects of the pressure indicators and the characteristics of policymaking for the three types of policy response.[16] The effects shown are maximum since the predictors have been rescaled to the 0–1 range.

As can be seen, both pressure and policymaking strongly affect the policy output at the national level. Regarding pressure, public salience has a powerful effect on the two more specific indicators – stringency and economic response: In line with H4c, political pressure greatly facilitates policy output. In the COVID-19 crisis, public attention is focused on the existential threat of the pandemic. The public expects the government to do something about this threat, and the government's response is immediate (with one week's lag). The effect on the overall response indicator is less pronounced, which may be attributed to this indicator's lower precision and the broad characterization of policymaking (across all policy domains). Controlling for public salience, problem pressure as measured by new weekly deaths also has a considerable impact on stringency

---

[16] Table A5 in the online Appendix provides the detailed results of the xtpmg analysis. The results shown are based on a dynamic panel analysis and refer to the pooled mean country effects across the six countries for which we have data across all the three waves. Unit root tests show that all time-series included in the analysis are stationary.

measures but a lower impact on the overall response and no impact on the economic response. Its effect is, to a large extent, mediated by public salience.

Controlling for external pressure, the policymaking characteristic with the most significant impact on the policy output for all three indicators is the salience of policymaking: It dramatically increases the policy response. Executive dominance weakly contributes to lockdown measures and slightly to the overall response but not to the economic response. However, policy support does not affect the three output indicators, contradicting the general hypothesis H4. This is to say that national policy output during the COVID-19 crisis directly resulted from the intensity with which policymakers dealt with the crisis and, to a limited extent, of prevailing executive actors. However, increasing levels of support among policymakers have not facilitated it. At first sight, this result may surprise. But it seems more plausible on reflection, as already discussed in the theory chapter. First of all, as we have seen throughout this study, policymaking during the COVID-19 crisis was rather consensual, i.e., under the tremendous exogenous pressure, policymakers rallied around the governments. The level of consensus was comparatively high throughout the crisis, and the partisan politicization of policymaking remained relatively limited. The limited variation in support of the government's proposals throughout the crisis is illustrated by Figure 24,

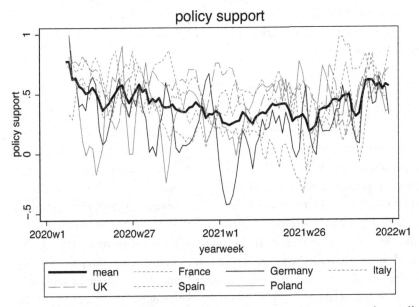

Figure 24 Time line of policy support in member states, by country and overall mean. The indicators have been smoothed by running averages over three weeks.

which presents the time lines for policy support. As this figure shows, on average, policy support is always positive. The average varies rather little across time, even if, as we have already seen (Figure 20), support varies across countries and sometimes even turns negative in countries such as Poland or Germany. As we have seen in Section 4 (Figure 5), the salience of policymaking is much more variable, on average, and its variation is more closely reflected in the policy output indicators. Moreover, as argued previously, exogenous pressure may force executive policymakers to come up with a response, even if broad sections of the political elite do not support them. To the extent that there was resistance against the government's policies in the COVID-19 crisis, resistance mainly targeted the lockdown measures (Kriesi and Oana 2023), it did not affect policy output. In the face of the enormous problem pressure and the equally vast pressure exerted by public opinion, the governments had little maneuvering room for taking the resistance exerted by specific groups into account.

Analyzing the determinants of policy output by wave (combining the second and third waves) for the *stringency* indicator, we find that problem pressure and public salience constitute the strongest determinants of lockdown measures in both waves (see Figure 25.)[17] This finding confirms the notion that the continued pressure kept up policy output during the COVID-19 crisis. Moreover, during the first wave, policy output was only a function of the effect of pressure, which is to say that early on in the COVID-19 crisis, policymakers at the national level just reacted to the pressure exerted by the crisis situation. In later waves, the salience of policymaking and the dominance of executive actors also played a role, but policy support remained insignificant.

Conclusion

The two crises differed markedly regarding policy output: At both levels of the EU polity, it was much more positive and consequential in the COVID-19 crisis than in the refugee crisis. This difference is primarily a result of the different crisis situations. In the COVID-19 crisis, the combination of overwhelming problem pressure and pressure from public opinion made for immediate and robust responses on the part of the leading actors. The other policymakers broadly supported this response, and even if they did not support it, the resistance was not very vocal, and the top policymakers could overcome it (at the EU level) or ignore it (at the national level). In contrast, in the refugee crisis, the strong opposition at the EU level led to the failure of the preferred solution in the short run and the inability to reform the asylum policy in the long run. At the

---

[17] Table A6 in the online Appendix provides the detailed results of the corresponding xtpmg analysis.

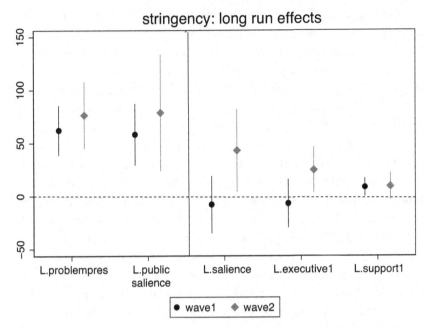

Figure 25 Determinants of policy output during the COVID-19 crisis for stringency indicator, by wave: long-run effects.

national level, the highly conflictual situation did not allow significant reforms either, leading mainly to symbolic politics. But, more fundamentally, the crisis exacerbated the conflict between nationalists and cosmopolitans, leading to a rightward shift in the party system with lasting consequences for national and EU politics.

7 Conclusion

Crises are critical junctures in which the alternative paths to the status quo – and the status quo preserving forces – become visible, even if other paths are not taken (Capoccia and Kelemen 2007; Schelkle 2021). Like wars, they can legitimize the buildup of centralized administrative, fiscal, and coercive capacities to deal with external threats (Freudlsperger and Schimmelfennig 2022). However, not all crises enhance capacity building at the center, and even the same crisis can simultaneously have centralizing and decentralizing implications. In this study, I have compared policymaking processes in two exogenous crises to clarify the link between the crisis situation and the outcome. I have sought to corroborate a deterministic thesis claiming that the crisis situation decisively shapes crisis-specific politics and policymaking, determining the policy output and effectiveness.

The analysis has shown that crisis policymaking has been both similar and different across the two crises. On the one hand, the critical juncture of a crisis has given rise to similar responses in the COVID-19 and the refugee crisis. In both crises, crisis-specific policymaking greatly increased once the exogenous shock hit. It responded primarily to the political pressure resulting from the crisis; the effect of problem pressure on the intensity of policymaking was more limited and indirect. Policymaking changed from parallel into serial mode and focused on the immediate threat of the crisis. Although this effect was characteristic of both crises, the shift to crisis policymaking was particularly impressive in the COVID-19 crisis – a result of the existential character, novelty, and broad scope of this threat. Second, in both crises, executive decision-making was enhanced. EU authorities and member state governments dominated policymaking at the EU level; governments prevailed at the national level. And to the extent that executive actors controlled the policymaking process at the national level during these crises, support for the government's proposal was generally enhanced. Third, at the origin of both crises, EU-level policymaking became much more salient than policymaking at the member-state level, suggesting that, during crises, EU authorities are called upon to rescue some or all member states. In a nutshell, crises generally tend to crowd out policymaking unrelated to the immediate threat they exert on the polity; they tend to reinforce the executive decision-making mode, and they tend to shift policymaking to the EU level.

On the other hand, differences between the two crises prevail regarding policy support and policy output. The COVID-19 crisis was much more consensual than the refugee crisis. All types of actors supported the policy proposals more during the COVID-19 than during the refugee crisis. Its more consensual character primarily results from its more symmetric, existential, and broad incidence. In addition, the limited partisan politicization and the limited extent to which politicization spilled across levels of the EU polity contributed to the "enabling consensus" during the COVID-19 crisis. At the EU level, consensual policymaking was also facilitated by the high competence of EU authorities in economic policy. However, in fiscal policy, where the EU competence was more limited, political resistance from transnational coalitions became more vocal even in this crisis. But it was overcome eventually by the joint effort of the leading German–French coalition and the southern European solidarity coalition. In public health policy, the shock of the crisis allowed for capacity building in a domain where the EU originally had almost no competence. At the national level, combined problem pressure and public salience enhanced policy support in the COVID-19 crisis but not in the refugee crisis. Surprisingly, however, this improved policy support did not affect policy output. Instead, policy output depended directly on both problem and political pressure in national policymaking during the COVID-19 crisis. This absence of any effect of policy support on policy output is probably the most pertinent evidence for the claim that the crisis situation decisively shapes policymaking during a crisis. If pressure is sufficiently strong, it allows leading policymakers to ignore opposition to its proposals. In contrast, during the refugee crisis, policymaking was highly conflictual at both levels of the EU polity, and the politicization at the two levels was interlinked. At the EU level, transnational coalitions came to prevent the preferred solutions; at the national level, partisan politicization loomed large, and political entrepreneurs exploited the crisis for their political purposes, loosening the link between problem and political pressure and policy output and, thus, preventing long-term policy solutions.

The analysis has also shown that crises are not necessarily unified entities. Some crises, such as the COVID-19 crisis, have a broad scope that concerns multiple policy domains. Depending on the distribution of competencies between the EU and its member states, the relative importance of EU authorities and governments varied not only by crisis but also by policy domain within the COVID-19 crisis – a more significant role for EU actors in economic and monetary policymaking, a more substantial role of the governments (the German–French coalition in particular) in the fiscal policy domain during the same crisis, and the refugee crisis more generally (especially the German and V4 governments). At the national level, the types of actors who played a central role in addition to the governments varied considerably between the crises: EU-polity actors and parties in the refugee crisis versus local–regional governments, experts, and civil society actors in the COVID-19 crisis.

There have been intense discussions about the applicability of the grand theories of European integration to the analysis of the two crises I have compared (e.g., Ferrara and Kriesi 2022; Hooghe and Marks 2019; Jones, Daniel Kelemen, and Meunier 2021; Schimmelfennig 2018). These discussions attempt to elucidate the *differences* between crises but do not have much to say about the similarities in EU policymaking across crises. Moreover, they are oblivious to policy domain-specific differences in policymaking within crises since they compare crises as a whole. Regarding their focus on the differences in policymaking between crises, they do not sufficiently appreciate that these differences result from the differences in the crisis situation. Hooghe and Marks (2019: 1117) point out that "[n]eofunctionalism and intergovernmental-ism conceive European integration as a cooperative process among interest groups and governments ... Postfunctionalism, by contrast, conceives European integration as a conflictual process arising from incompatible belief systems." These contrasting perceptions of the integration process make the former more likely to account for policymaking during the COVID-19 pandemic, which was characterized by an "enabling consensus," and the latter more likely to account for policymaking during the refugee crisis, which was characterized by a "constraining dissensus" (Ferrara and Kriesi 2022). Jones, Daniel Kelemen, and Meunier (2021) specify "scope conditions" for the applicability of their approach. Ferrara and Kriesi (2022) highlight that the applicability of a given theory depends on critical aspects of the crisis situation. In line with the latters' reasoning, the present study suggests that, instead of an eclectic application of integration theories depending on the "scope conditions," it would be most appropriate to consider these "scope conditions," defined by the crisis situation, as the key explanatory factors on which not only the applicability of the various integration theories but above all the understanding of the policymaking process depends.

In contrast, the literature on public policy, crisis management, and emergency politics put into evidence the *similarities* across crises. Thus, the punctuated equilibrium approach focuses on the punctuation, i.e., the crisis period in public policymaking. In the crisis management literature, Rhinard (2019) suggests that policymaking dynamics in the EU have generally undergone a process of "crisisification," which includes "a determined focus on finding the next urgent event" and "a prioritization of speed in decision-making" (p. 629). According to this claim, politicians are in "search for crises" (p. 624) and pursue a "security logic." Related to this claim, White (2020) identifies the ascendancy of a new governing mode centered on the logic of emergency in the EU. According to White, this new governing mode is independent of the specifics of a particular context. It is linked to an informalization, de-institutionalization, and personalization of power. In the EU, power has come to be diffused across many executive institutions, undermining the capacity for decisive action and opening up the possibility for ad hoc centralization of power to deal with exceptional situations (p. 56). The underlying assumption seems to be that executive actors have explicitly pursued this development to aggrandize their power.

The results of the present study confirm the increasing role of executive decision-making during crises and the functional pressure for an immediate policy response. In line with White's (2020: 135) claim, transnational emergency rule represents the intensification of governing by the principle of necessity, or TINA ("There is no alternative"). However, according to the results of the present study, executive actors do not resort to this kind of governing by choice. If anything, they fail to anticipate the coming emergency and are trapped by the emergency, events forcing their hand. As Machiavelli (cited by White 2020: 56) pointed out a long time ago: "The worst defect weak republics can have is to be indecisive, so that all their decisions are taken out of necessity, and if any good comes to them, it comes through force of circumstance rather than through their own prudence" (Discourses I, 38: p. 103). Rather than emergency politics, the defect of EU policymaking is the lack of foresight and established procedures to deal with emergencies effectively. This conclusion applies to all crises, not only to the exogenous shock-type crises that we have studied here, but even more so to erosion-type crises such as climate change, the social security crisis, or the geopolitical security (Ukrainian war) crisis, which come about slowly and cumulatively and which could be anticipated by policymakers.

References

Aberbach, Joel D., Robert D. Putnam, Bert A. Rockmann et al. 1981. *Bureaucrats and Politicians in Western Democracies*. Cambridge, MA: Harvard University Press.

Abou-Chadi, Tarik, Denis Cohen, and Markus Wagner. 2021. "The Centre-Right versus the Radical Right: The Role of Migration Issues and Economic Grievances." *Journal of Ethnic and Migration Studies* 42(2): 366–84. https://doi.org/10.1080/1369183X.2020.1853903.

Abou-Chadi, Tarik, and Werner Krause. 2020. "The Causal Effect of Radical Right Success on Mainstream Parties' Policy Positions: A Regression Discontinuity Approach." *British Journal of Political Science* 50(3): 829–47. https://doi.org/10.1017/S0007123418000029.

Alexander, Robin. 2021. *Machtverfall. Merkels Ende Und Das Drama Der Deutschen Politik: Ein Report*. München: Siedler.

Alexander Shaw, Kate, Daniel Kovarek, and Waltraud Schelkle. 2024. "Explaining 'Good' and 'Bad' Crises in and for the EU."

Alexander-Shaw, Kate, Joseph Ganderson, and Anna Kyriazi. 2023. "Mapping Crisis Contestations: Taking Constructions Seriously in the Age of Permanent Crisis." Unpublished manuscript.

Altiparmakis, Argyrios, Abel Bojar, Sylvain Brouard et al. 2021. "Pandemic Politics: Policy Evaluations of Government Responses to COVID-19." *West European Politics* 44(5–6): 1159–79. https://doi.org/10.1080/01402382.2021.1930754.

Anghel, Veronica, and Erik Jones. 2023. "Is Europe Really Forged through Crisis? Pandemic EU and the Russia – Ukraine War." *Journal of European Public Policy* 30(4): 766–86. https://doi.org/10.1080/13501763.2022.2140820.

Baekgaard, Martin, Julian Christensen, Jonas Krogh Madsen, and Kim Sass Mikkelsen. 2020. "Rallying around the Flag in Times of COVID-19: Societal Lockdown and Trust in Democratic Institutions." *Journal of Behavioral Public Administration* 3(2). https://doi.org/10.30636/jbpa.32.172.

Bartolini, Stefano. 2005. *Restructuring Europe: Centre Formation, System Building, and Political Structuring between the Nation State and the European Union*. Oxford: Oxford University Press.

Baumgartner, Frank R., and Bryan D. Jones. 2002. *Policy Dynamics*. Chicago: University of Chicago Press.

Baumgartner, Frank R., Bryan D. Jones, and Peter B. Mortensen. 2014. "Punctuated Equilibrium Theory: Explaining Stability and Change in Public Policymaking." In *Theories of the Policy Process*, eds. Paul A. Sabatier and Christopher M. Weible. Boulder: Westview Press, 59–103.

Baumgartner, Frank R., Christian Breunig, and Emiliano Grossman. 2019. "The Comparative Agendas Project : Intellectual Roots and Current Developments." https://kops.uni-konstanz.de/handle/123456789/45982 (February 23, 2024).

Baumgartner, Frank R., Christoffer Green-Pedersen, and Bryan D. Jones. 2006. "Comparative Studies of Policy Agendas." *Journal of European Public Policy* 13(7): 959–74.

Becker, Manuel, and Thomas Gehring. 2023. "Explaining EU Integration Dynamics in the Wake of COVID-19: A Domain of Application Approach." *Journal of European Public Policy* 30(2): 334–53. https://doi.org/10.1080/13501763.2022.2027000.

Bermeo, Nancy. 2016. "On Democratic Backsliding." *Journal of Democracy* 27(1): 5–19. https://doi.org/10.1353/jod.2016.0012.

Bickerton, Christopher J. 2012. *European Integration : From Nation-States to Member States*. 1st ed. Oxford University Press.

Bickerton, Christopher, Dermot Hodson, and Uwe Puetter. 2015. "The New Intergovernmentalism and the Study of European Integration." In *The New Intergovernmentalism*, eds. Christopher Bickerton, Dermot Hodson, and Uwe Puetter. Oxford: Oxford University Press, 1–48.

Biermann, Felix, Guérin, Nina, Jagdhuber, Stefan, Rittberger, Berthold, and Weiss, Moritz (2017). Political (Non-)reform in the Euro Crisis and the Refugee Crisis: A Liberal Intergovernmentalist Explanation. *Journal of European Public Policy*, 26(2): 246–66. https://doi.org/10.1080/13501763.2017.1408670

Birkland, Thomas A. 2009. "Disasters, Lessons Learned, and Fantasy Documents." *Journal of Contingencies and Crisis Management* 17(3): 146–56. https://doi.org/10.1111/j.1468-5973.2009.00575.x.

Boeri, Tito, and Roberto Perotti. 2023. *PNRR: la grande abbuffata*. Prima edizione in "Varia." Milano: Feltrinelli.

Bohle, Dorothee, Béla Greskovits, and Marek Naczyk. 2023. "The Gramscian Politics of Europe's Rule of Law Crisis." *Journal of European Public Policy* 31(7): 1775–1798. https://doi.org/10.1080/13501763.2023.2182342.

Boin, Arjen, Paul 't Hart, and Allan McConnell. 2009. "Crisis Exploitation: Political and Policy Impacts of Framing Contests." *Journal of European Public Policy* 16(1): 81–106. https://doi.org/10.1080/13501760802453221.

Boin, Arjen, Paul t'Hart, Eric Stern, and Bengt Sundelius. 2005. *The Politics of Crisis Management Public Leadership under Pressure.* Cambridge: Cambridge University Press.

Bojar, Abel, and Hanspeter Kriesi. 2023. "Policymaking in the EU under Crisis Conditions: Covid and Refugee Crises Compared." *Comparative European Politics* 21(4): 427–47. doi:10.1057/s41295-023-00349-1.

Bojar, Abel, Anna Kyriazi, Ioana-Elena Oana, and Zbigniew Truchlewski. 2023. *A Novel Method for Studying Policymaking: Policy Process Analysis (PPA) Applied to the Refugee Crisis.* European University Institute. Working Paper, 2023/24. https://cadmus.eui.eu/handle/1814/75543 (May 11, 2023).

Bojar, Abel, and Hanspeter Kriesi. 2021. "Action Repertoires in Contentious Episodes: What Determines Governments' and Challengers' Action Strategies? A Cross-national Analysis." *European Journal of Political Research* 60(1): 46–68. https://doi.org/10.1111/1475-6765.12386.

Bojar, Abel, Theresa Gessler, Swen Hutter, and Hanspeter Kriesi. 2021. *Contentious Episodes in the Age of Austerity: Studying the Dynamics of Government-Challenger Interactions.* Cambridge: Cambridge University Press.

Bol, Damien, Marco Giani, André Blais, and Peter John Loewen. 2021. "The Effect of COVID-19 Lockdowns on Political Support: Some Good News for Democracy?" *European Journal of Political Research* 60(2): 497–505. https://doi.org/10.1111/1475-6765.12401.

Bolleyer, Nicole, and Orsolya Salát. 2021. "Parliaments in Times of Crisis: COVID-19, Populism and Executive Dominance." *West European Politics* 44(5–6): 1103–28. https://doi.org/10.1080/01402382.2021.1930733.

Bornschier, Simon. 2010. *Cleavage Politics and the Populist Right: The New Cultural Conflict in Western Europe.* Philadelphia: Temple University Press.

Capoccia, Giovanni, and R. Daniel Kelemen. 2007. "The Study of Critical Junctures: Theory, Narrative, and Counterfactuals in Historical Institutionalism." *World Politics* 59 (3): 341–69. https://doi.org/10.1017/S0043887100020852.

De Vries, Catherine E., and Sara B. Hobolt. 2020. *Political Entrepreneurs: The Rise of Challenger Parties in Europe.* Princeton: Princeton University Press.

Earl, Jennifer, Andrew Martin, John D. McCarthy, and Sarah A. Soule. 2004. "The Use of Newspaper Data in the Study of Collective Action." *Annual Review of Sociology* 30(1): 65–80. https://doi.org/10.1146/annurev.soc.30.012703.110603.

Eichenberger, Steven, Frédéric Varone, Pascal Sciarini, Robin Stähli, and Jessica Proulx. 2023. "When Do Decision Makers Listen (Less) to Experts? The Swiss Government's Implementation of Scientific Advice during the

COVID-19 Crisis." *Policy Studies Journal* 51(3): 587–605. https://doi.org/10.1111/psj.12494.

Engler, Fabian, Svenja Bauer-Blaschkowski, and Reimut Zohlnhöfer. 2019. "Disregarding the Voters? Electoral Competition and the Merkel Government's Public Policies, 2013–17." *German Politics* 28(3): 312–31. https://doi.org/10.1080/09644008.2018.1495709.

Esaiasson, Peter, Jacob Sohlberg, Marina Ghersetti, and Bengt Johansson. 2021. "How the Coronavirus Crisis Affects Citizen Trust in Institutions and in Unknown Others: Evidence from 'the Swedish Experiment.'" *European Journal of Political Research* 60(3): 748–60. https://doi.org/10.1111/1475-6765.12419.

Fabbrini, Sergio. 2019. *Europe's Future: Decoupling and Reforming.* Cambridge: Cambridge University Press.

Fabbrini, Federico. 2022. "The Legal Architecture of the Economic Responses to COVID-19: EMU beyond the Pandemic*." *JCMS: Journal of Common Market Studies* 60(1): 186–203. https://doi.org/10.1111/jcms.13271.

Fabbrini, Sergio. 2023. "Going beyond the Pandemic: 'Next Generation Eu' and the Politics of Sub-Regional Coalitions." *Comparative European Politics* 21(1): 64–81. https://doi.org/10.1057/s41295-022-00302-8.

Ferrera, Maurizio, Anna Kyriazi, and Joan Miró. 2022. "Integration through Expansive Unification: The Birth of the European Health Union." *unpubl. paper.*

Ferrara, Federico Maria, and Hanspeter Kriesi. 2022. "Crisis Pressures and European Integration." *Journal of European Public Policy* 29(9): 1351–73. https://doi.org/10.1080/13501763.2021.1966079.

Ferrera, Maurizio, Hanspeter Kriesi, and Waltraud Schelkle. 2024. "Maintaining the EU's Compound Polity during the Long Crisis Decade." *Journal of European Public Policy* 31(3): 706–28. https://doi.org/10.1080/13501763.2023.2165698.

Ferrera, Maurizio, Joan Miró, and Stefano Ronchi. 2021. "Walking the Road Together? EU Polity Maintenance during the COVID-19 Crisis." *West European Politics* 44(5–6): 1–24. https://doi.org/10.1080/01402382.2021.1905328.

Freudlsperger, Christian, and Frank Schimmelfennig. 2022. "Transboundary Crises and Political Development: Why War Is Not Necessary for European State-Building." *Journal of European Public Policy* 29(12): 1871–84. https://doi.org/10.1080/13501763.2022.2141822.

Geddes, Andrew. 2018. "The Politics of European Union Migration Governance: EU Migration Governance." *JCMS: Journal of Common Market Studies* 56: 120–30. https://doi.org/10.1111/jcms.12763.

Geddes, Andrew. 2021. *Governing Migration beyond the State: Europe, North America, South America and Southeast Asia in a Global Context*. Oxford: Oxford University Press.

Geddes, Andrew, Leila Hadj Abdou, and Leiza Brumat. 2020. *Migration and Mobility in the European Union*. 2nd ed. London: Macmillan Education.

Genschel, Philipp, and Markus Jachtenfuchs. 2018. "From Market Integration to Core State Powers: The Eurozone Crisis, the Refugee Crisis and Integration Theory: Crises in Core State Powers." *JCMS: Journal of Common Market Studies* 56(1): 178–96. https://doi.org/10.1111/jcms.12654.

Genschel, Philipp, and Markus Jachtenfuchs. 2021. "Postfunctionalism Reversed: Solidarity and Rebordering during the COVID-19 Pandemic." *Journal of European Public Policy* 28(3): 350–69. https://doi.org/10.1080/13501763.2021.1881588.

Gruber, Oliver. 2017. "'Refugees (No Longer) Welcome'. Asylum Discourse and Policy in Austria in the Wake of the 2015 Refugee Crisis." In *The Migrant Crisis: European Perspectives and National Discourses*, eds. Melanie Barlai, Birte Fähnrich, Christina Griessler, and Markus Rhomberg. Zürich: Lit-Verlag, 39–57.

Hix, Simon, and Björn Hoyland. 2022. *The Political System of the European Union*. 4th ed. London: Bloomsbury PLC.

Hobolt, Sara B., and Catherine E. de Vries. 2015. "Issue Entrepreneurship and Multiparty Competition." *Comparative Political Studies* 48(9): 1159–85. https://doi.org/10.1177/0010414015575030.

Höhmann, Daniel, and Ulrich Sieberer. 2020. "Parliamentary Questions as a Control Mechanism in Coalition Governments." *West European Politics* 43(1): 225–49. https://doi.org/10.1080/01402382.2019.1611986.

Hooghe, Liesbet, and Gary Marks. 2018. "Cleavage Theory Meets Europe's Crises: Lipset, Rokkan, and the Transnational Cleavage." *Journal of European Public Policy* 25(1): 109–35. https://doi.org/10.1080/13501763.2017.1310279.

Hooghe, Liesbet, and Gary Marks. 2019. "Grand Theories of European Integration in the Twenty-First Century." *Journal of European Public Policy* 26(8): 1113–33. https://doi.org/10.1080/13501763.2019.1569711.

Hooghe, Liesbet, Gary Marks, and Carole J. Wilson. 2002. "Does Left/Right Structure Party Positions on European Integration?" *Comparative Political Studies* 35(8): 965–89. https://doi.org/10.1177/001041402236310.

Hutter, Swen. 2014. "Protest Event Analysis and Its Offspring." In *Methodological Practices in Social Movement Research*, ed. Donatella Della Porta. Oxford: Oxford University Press, 335–67.

Jones, Erik, R. Daniel Kelemen, and Sophie Meunier. 2021. "Failing Forward? Crises and Patterns of European Integration." *Journal of European Public Policy* 28(10): 1519–36. https://doi.org/10.1080/13501763.2021.1954068.

Junk, Wiebke Marie, Michele Crepaz, Marcel Hanegraaff, Joost Berkhout, and Ellis Aizenberg. 2022. "Changes in Interest Group Access in Times of Crisis: No Pain, No (Lobby) Gain." *Journal of European Public Policy* 29(9): 1374–94. https://doi.org/10.1080/13501763.2021.1968936.

Koopmans, Ruud, and Paul Statham. 1999. "Political Claims Analysis: Integrating Protest Event and Political Discourse Approaches." *Mobilization: An International Quarterly* 4(2): 203–21. https://doi.org/10.17813/maiq.4.2.d759337060716756.

Kriesi, Hanspeter, Abel Bojar, Argyrios Altiparmakis, and Ioana-Elena Oana. 2024. *Coming to Terms with the European Refugee Crisis*. Cambridge: Cambridge University Press.

Kriesi, Hanspeter, and Alina Vrânceanu. 2023. "Voter Preferences for EU Asylum Policies: The Role of Government Cues." *Government and Opposition*: 1–23. https://doi.org/10.1017/gov.2023.41.

Kriesi, Hanspeter, Argyrios Altiparmakis, Abel Bojar, and Ioana-Elena Oana. 2021. "Debordering and Re-Bordering in the Refugee Crisis: A Case of 'Defensive Integration.'" *Journal of European Public Policy* 28(3): 331–49. https://doi.org/10.1080/13501763.2021.1882540.

Kriesi, Hanspeter, Edgar Grande, Martin Dolezal, Marc Helbling, Dominic Höglinger, Swen Hutter, and Bruno Wüest. 2012. *Political Conflict in Western Europe*. Cambridge: Cambridge University Press.

Kriesi, Hanspeter, Edgar Grande, Romain Lachat et al. 2008. *West European Politics in the Age of Globalization*. Cambridge: Cambridge University Press.

Kriesi, Hanspeter, and Ioana-Elena Oana. 2023. "Protest in Unlikely Times: Dynamics of Collective Mobilization in Europe during the COVID-19 Crisis." *Journal of European Public Policy* 30(4): 740–65. https://doi.org/10.1080/13501763.2022.2140819.

Krotz, Ulrich, and Lucas Schramm. 2022. "Embedded Bilateralism, Integration Theory, and European Crisis Politics: France, Germany, and the Birth of the EU Corona Recovery Fund*." *JCMS: Journal of Common Market Studies* 60(3): 526–44. https://doi.org/10.1111/jcms.13251.

Ladi, Stella, and Sarah Wolff. 2021. "The EU Institutional Architecture in the Covid-19 Response: Coordinative Europeanization in Times of Permanent Emergency." *JCMS: Journal of Common Market Studies* 59(S1): 32–43. https://doi.org/10.1111/jcms.13254.

Laffan, Brigid. 2023. "Escaping the Politics Trap: Exercising Collective Power." In Florence: EUI. Unpublished paper.

Laffan, Brigid, and Stefan Telle. 2023. *The EU's Response to Brexit: United and Effective*. London: Palgrave Macmillan.

Lavazza, Andrea, and Mirko Farina. 2020. "The Role of Experts in the Covid-19 Pandemic and the Limits of Their Epistemic Authority in Democracy." *Frontiers in Public Health* 8: 356. https://doi.org/10.3389/fpubh.2020.00356.

Lavenex, Sandra. 2018. "'Failing Forward' Towards Which Europe? Organized Hypocrisy in the Common European Asylum System." *JCMS: Journal of Common Market Studies* 56(5): 1195–1212. https://doi.org/10.1111/jcms.12739.

Lipscy, Phillip Y. 2020. "COVID-19 and the Politics of Crisis." *International Organization* 74(S1): E98–E127. https://doi.org/10.1017/S0020818320000375.

Louwerse, Tom, Ulrich Sieberer, Or Tuttnauer, and Rudy B. Andeweg. 2021. "Opposition in Times of Crisis: COVID-19 in Parliamentary Debates." *West European Politics* 44(5–6): 1025–51. https://doi.org/10.1080/01402382.2021.1886519.

Maor, Moshe, and Michael Howlett. 2020. "Explaining Variations in State COVID-19 Responses: Psychological, Institutional, and Strategic Factors in Governance and Public Policy-Making." *Policy Design and Practice* 3(3): 228–41. https://doi.org/10.1080/25741292.2020.1824379.

McKay, David. 2004. "William Riker on Federalism: Sometimes Wrong but More Right than Anybody Else?" *Regional and Federal Studies* 14(2): 167–86. https://doi.org/10.1080/1359756042000247438

van der Meer, Tom, Eefje Steenvoorden, and Ebe Ouattara. 2023. "Fear and the COVID-19 Rally Round the Flag: A Panel Study on Political Trust." *West European Politics* 46(6): 1089–1105. https://doi.org/10.1080/01402382.2023.2171220.

van Middelaar, Luuk. 2017. *De Nieuwe Politiek van Europa*. Brussels: Historische Uitgeverij.

van Middelaar, Luuk. 2019. *Alarums and Excursions: Improvising Politics on the European State*. Newcastle upon Tyne: Agenda.

Milward, Alan S. 2000. *The European Rescue of the Nation-State*. 2nd ed. London: Routledge.

Mistur, Evan M., John Wagner Givens, and Daniel C. Matisoff. 2023. "Contagious COVID-19 Policies: Policy Diffusion during Times of Crisis." *The Review of Policy Research* 40(1): 36–62. https://doi.org/10.1111/ropr.12487.

Monnet, Jean 1978. *Memoirs*. New York: Doubleday.

Moravcsik, Andrew. 1998. *The Choice for Europe: Social Purpose and State Power from Messina to Maastricht*. Ithaca, N.Y: Cornell University Press.

Mueller, John E. 1970. "Presidential Popularity from Truman to Johnson1." *American Political Science Review* 64(1): 18–34. https://doi.org/10.2307/1955610.

Niemann, Arne, and Johanna Speyer. 2018. "A Neofunctionalist Perspective on the 'European Refugee Crisis': The Case of the European Border and Coast

Guard." *JCMS: Journal of Common Market Studies* 56(1): 23–43. https://doi .org/10.1111/jcms.12653.

Ortiz, David, Daniel Myers, Eugene Walls, and Maria-Elena Diaz. 2006. "Where Do We Stand with Newspaper Data?" *Mobilization: An International Quarterly* 10(3): 397–419. https://doi.org/10.17813/maiq.10.3.8360r760k3277t42.

Pierson, Paul. 2004. *Politics in Time: History, Institutions, and Social Analysis*. Princeton: Princeton University Press.

Popic, Tamara, and Alexandru D. Moise. 2022. "Government Responses to the COVID-19 Pandemic in Eastern and Western Europe: The Role of Health, Political and Economic Factors." *East European Politics* 38(4): 507–28. https://doi.org/10.1080/21599165.2022.2122050.

Quaglia, Lucia, and Amy Verdun. 2023. "Explaining the Response of the ECB to the COVID-19 Related Economic Crisis: Inter-Crisis and Intra-Crisis Learning." *Journal of European Public Policy* 30(4): 635–54. https://doi .org/10.1080/13501763.2022.2141300.

Rauh, Christian, Bart Joachim Bes, and Martijn Schoonvelde. 2020. "Undermining, Defusing or Defending European Integration? Assessing Public Communication of European Executives in Times of EU Politicisation." *European Journal of Political Research* 59(2): 397–423. https://doi.org/10.1111/1475-6765.12350.

Rhinard, Mark. 2019. "The Crisisification of Policy-Making in the European Union." *JCMS: Journal of Common Market Studies* 57(3): 616–33. https:// doi.org/10.1111/jcms.12838.

Rhodes, Martin. 2021. "'Failing Forward': A Critique in Light of Covid-19." *Journal of European Public Policy* 28(10): 1537–54. https://doi.org/10.1080/ 13501763.2021.1954067.

Rovny, Jan, Ryan Bakker, Liesbet Hooghe et al. 2022. "Contesting Covid: The Ideological Bases of Partisan Responses to the Covid-19 Pandemic." *European Journal of Political Research* 61(4): 1155–64. https://doi.org/ 10.1111/1475-6765.12510.

Schattschneider, Elmer Eric. 1975. *The Semisovereign People: A Realist's View of Democracy in America*. Oak Brook, IL: Dryden Press.

Schelkle, Waltraud. 2021. "Fiscal Integration in an Experimental Union: How Path-Breaking Was the EU's Response to the COVID-19 Pandemic?" *JCMS: Journal of Common Market Studies* 59(S1): 44–55. https://doi.org/10.1111/jcms.13246.

Schimmelfennig, Frank. 2018. "Liberal Intergovernmentalism and the Crises of the European Union." *JCMS: Journal of Common Market Studies* 56(7): 1578–94. https://doi.org/10.1111/jcms.12789.

Schimmelfennig, Frank. 2021. "Rebordering Europe: External Boundaries and Integration in the European Union." *Journal of European Public Policy* 28(3): 311–30. https://doi.org/10.1080/13501763.2021.1881589.

Schmidt, Vivien A. 2022. "European Emergency Politics and the Question of Legitimacy." *Journal of European Public Policy* 29(6): 979–93. https://doi.org/10.1080/13501763.2021.1916061.

Schraff, Dominik. 2021. "Political Trust during the Covid-19 Pandemic: Rally around the Flag or Lockdown Effects?" *European Journal of Political Research* 60(4): 1007–17. https://doi.org/10.1111/1475-6765.12425.

Schramm, Lucas. 2023. "Economic Ideas, Party Politics, or Material Interests? Explaining Germany's Support for the EU Corona Recovery Plan." *Journal of European Public Policy* 30(1): 84–103. https://doi.org/10.1080/13501763.2021.1985592.

Seabrooke, Leonard, and Eleni Tsingou. 2019. "Europe's Fast-and Slow-Burning Crises." *Journal of European Public Policy* 26(3): 468–81. https://doi.org/10.1080/13501763.2018.1446456

Sebhatu, Abiel, Karl Wennberg, Stefan Arora-Jonsson, and Staffan I. Lindberg. 2020. "Explaining the Homogeneous Diffusion of COVID-19 Nonpharmaceutical Interventions across Heterogeneous Countries." *Proceedings of the National Academy of Sciences* 117(35): 21201–208. https://doi.org/10.1073/pnas.2010625117.

Thielemann, Eiko. 2018. "Why Refugee Burden-Sharing Initiatives Fail: Public Goods, Free-Riding and Symbolic Solidarity in the EU." *JCMS: Journal of Common Market Studies* 56(1): 63–82. https://doi.org/10.1111/jcms.12662.

Tilly, Charles. 1978. *From Mobilization to Revolution.* Reading, MA: Addison-Wesley.

Toshkov, Dimiter, Brendan Carroll, and Kutsal Yesilkagit. 2022. "Government Capacity, Societal Trust or Party Preferences: What Accounts for the Variety of National Policy Responses to the COVID-19 Pandemic in Europe?" *Journal of European Public Policy* 29(7): 1009–28. https://doi.org/10.1080/13501763.2021.1928270.

Truchlewski, Zbigniew, Ioana-Elena Oana, Alexandru D. Moise, and Hanspeter Kriesi. 2023. *Pandemic Polity-Building: How COVID-19 Shaped the European Union.* Florence: EUI: unpubl ms.

Verdun, Amy. 2022. "The Greatest of the Small? The Netherlands, the New Hanseatic League and the Frugal Four." *German Politics* 31(2): 302–22. https://doi.org/10.1080/09644008.2021.2003782.

Vries, Catherine E. De. 2017. "Benchmarking Brexit: How the British Decision to Leave Shapes EU Public Opinion." *JCMS: Journal of Common Market Studies* 55(S1): 38–53. https://doi.org/10.1111/jcms.12579.

Webber, Douglas. 2019. *European Disintegration?: The Politics of Crisis in the European Union*. New York: Red Globe Press.

Red Globe is an imprint of Springer Nature Limited.

White, Jonathan. 2020. *Politics of Last Resort Politics of Last Resort: Governing by Emergency in the European Union*. Oxford: Oxford University Press.

Wolff, Sarah, and Stella Ladi. 2020. "European Union Responses to the Covid-19 Pandemic: Adaptability in Times of Permanent Emergency." *Journal of European Integration* 42(8): 1025–40. https://doi.org/10.1080/07036337.2020.1853120.

Zaller, John. 1992. *The Nature and Origins of Mass Opinion*. Cambridge: Cambridge University Press.

Zürn, Michael, and Pieter de Wilde. 2016. "Debating Globalization: Cosmopolitanism and Communitarianism as Political Ideologies." *Journal of Political Ideologies* 21(3): 280–301. https://doi.org/10.1080/13569317.2016.1207741.

Acknowledgements

The research for this study and its publication have been supported by the ERC-Synergy project SOLID, No 810356. I want to thank my colleagues from the project, as well as two anonymous reviewers, for their critical comments on earlier versions of the manuscript, which undoubtedly helped improve it.

About the Series
The Cambridge Elements Series in European Politics will provide a platform for cutting-edge comparative research on Europe at a time of rapid change for the disciplines of political science and international relations. The series is broadly defined, both in terms of subject and academic discipline. The thrust of the series will be thematic rather than ideographic. It will focus on studies that engage key elements of politics – e.g. how institutions work, how parties compete, how citizens participate in politics, how laws get made.

Cambridge Elements ≡

European Politics

Elements in the Series

A full series listing is available at: www.cambridge.org/EEP

Printed in the United States
by Baker & Taylor Publisher Services